... I Love you Papa ...

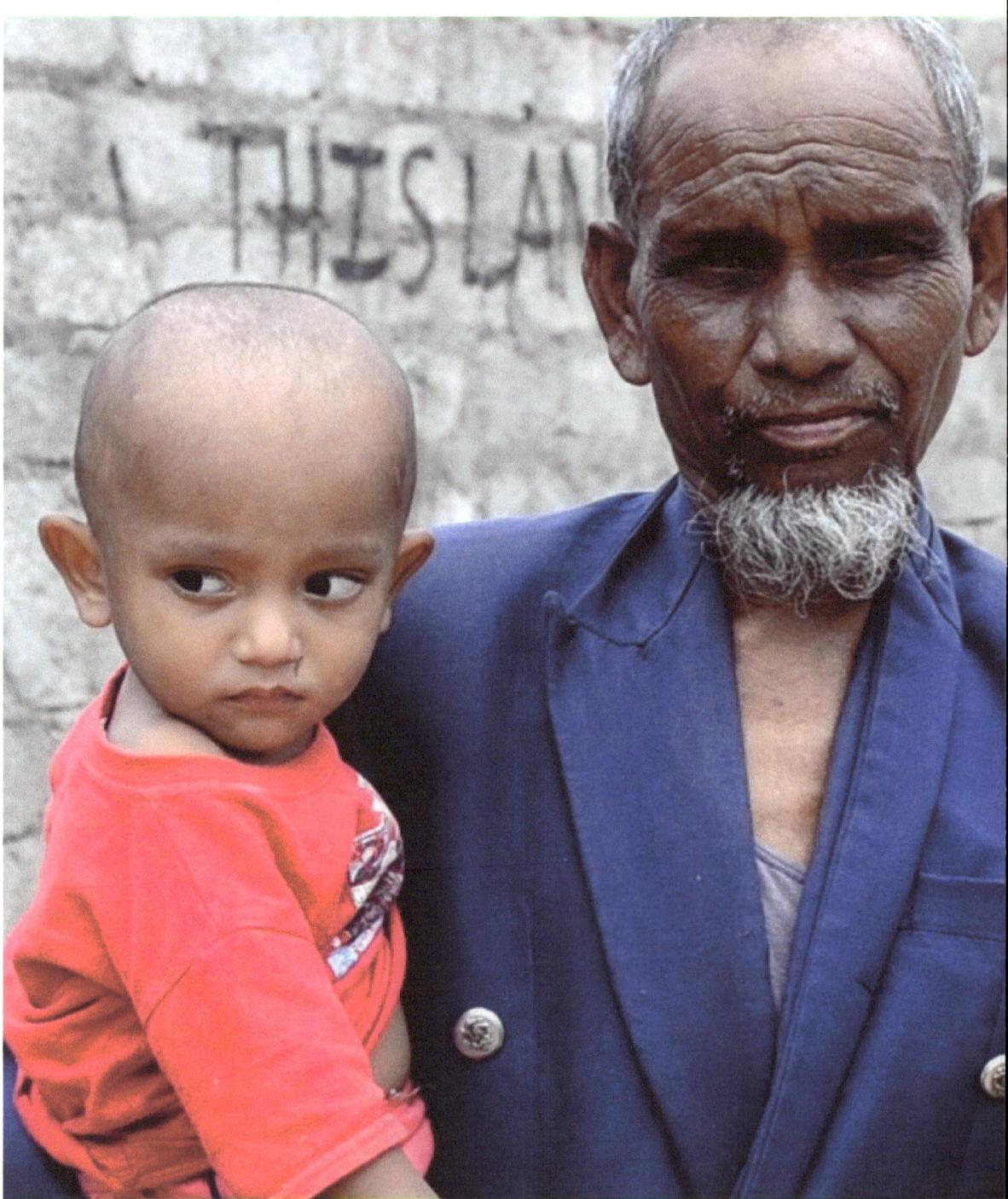

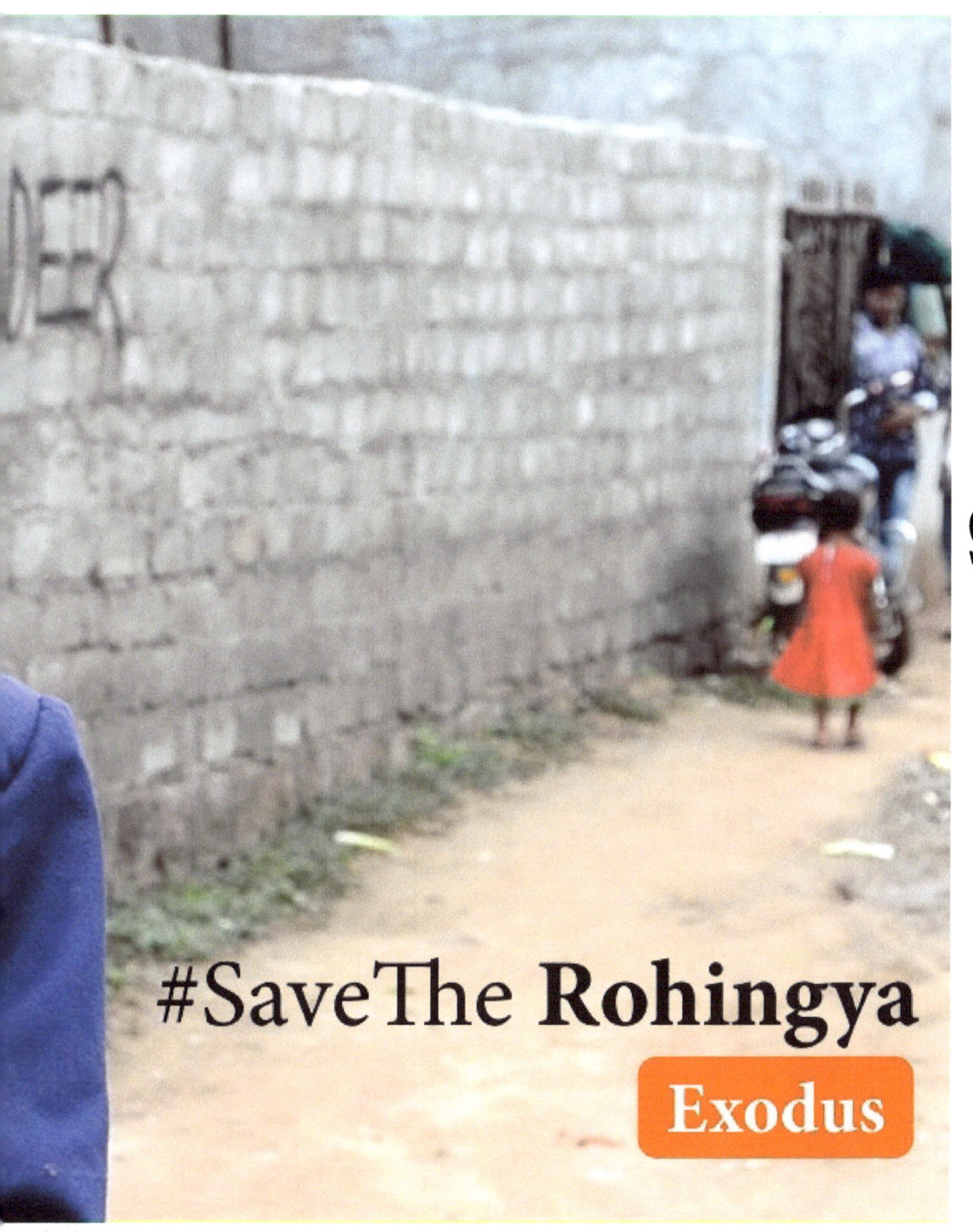

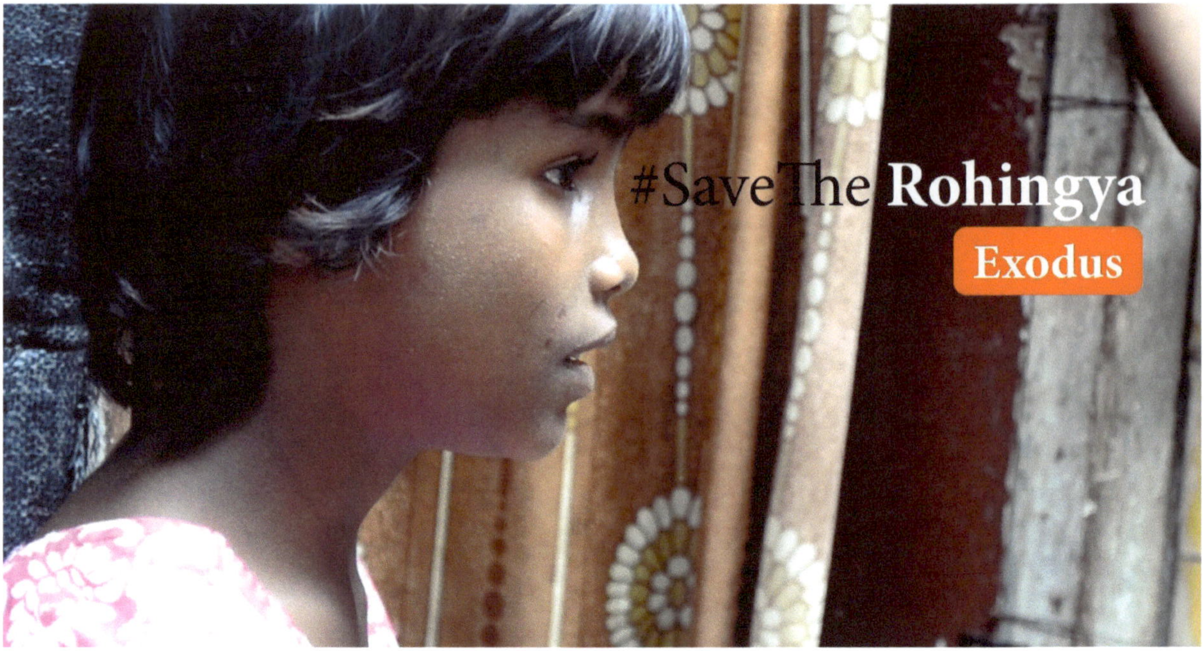

#SaveThe Rohingya
Exodus

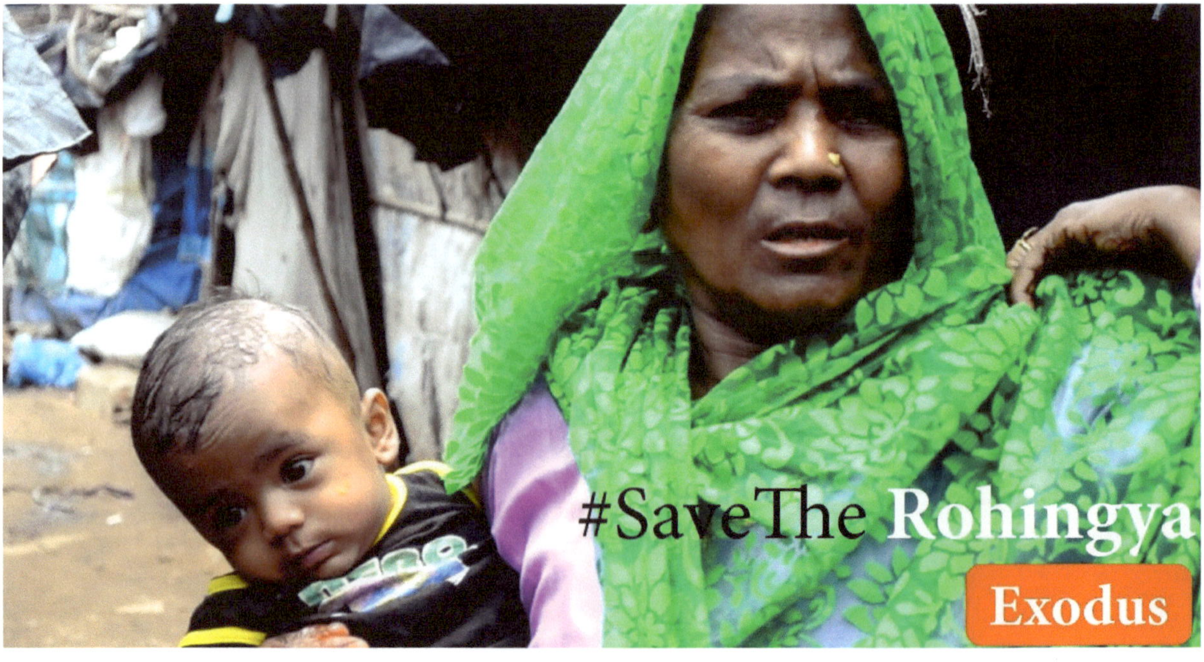

#SaveThe Rohingya
Exodus

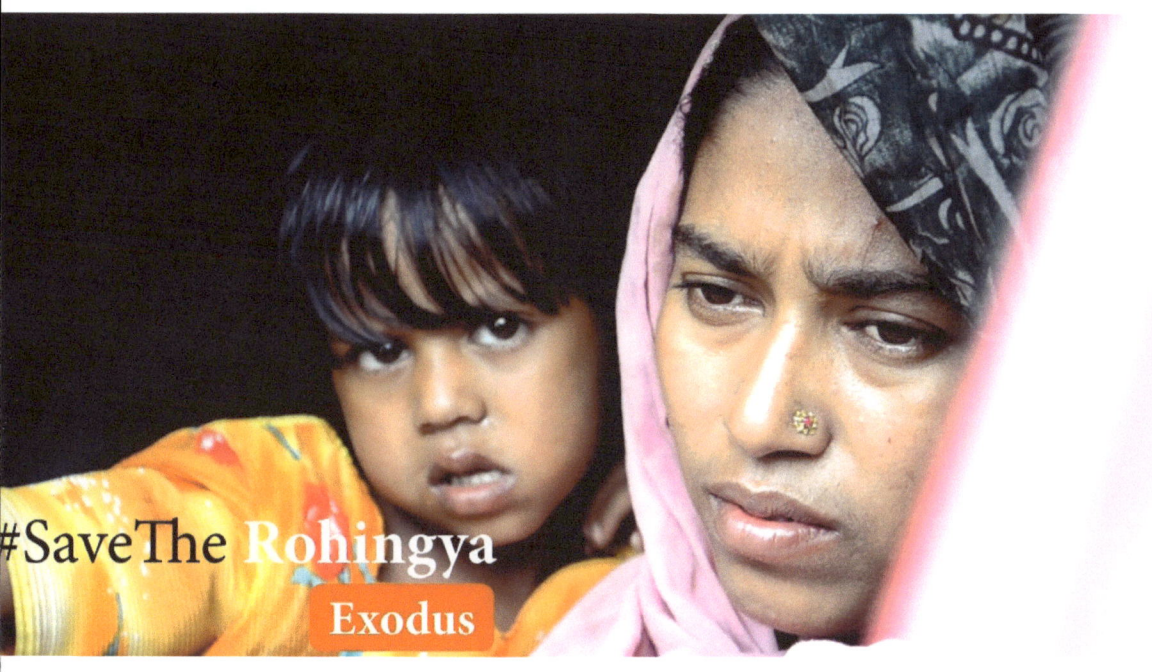
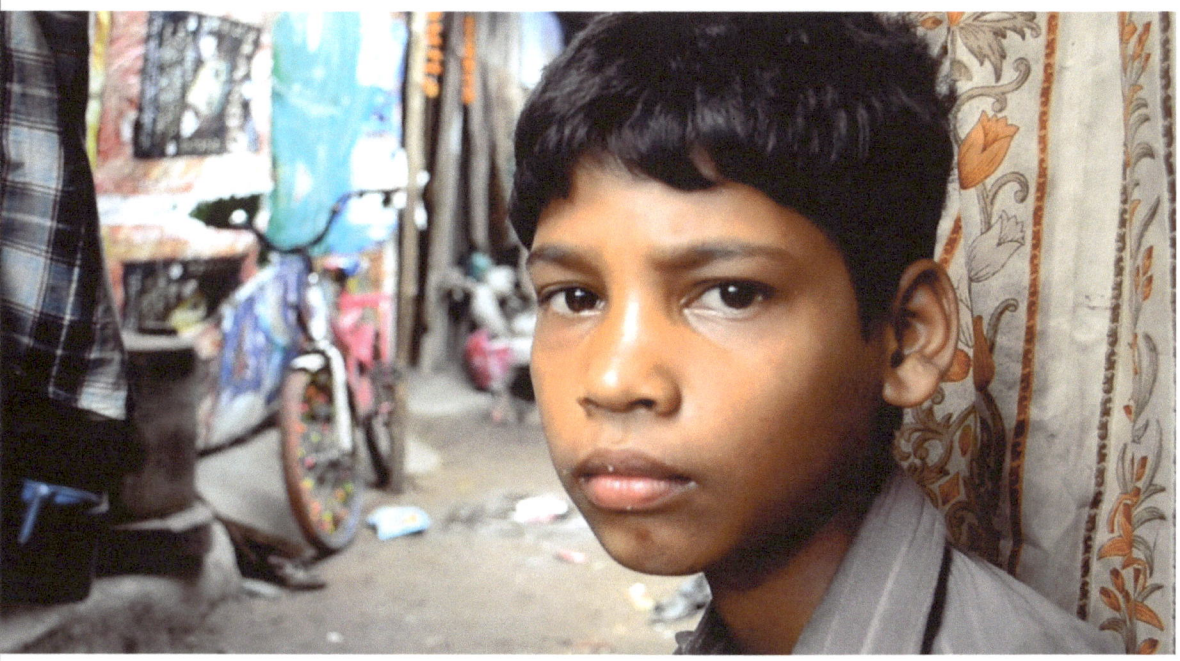

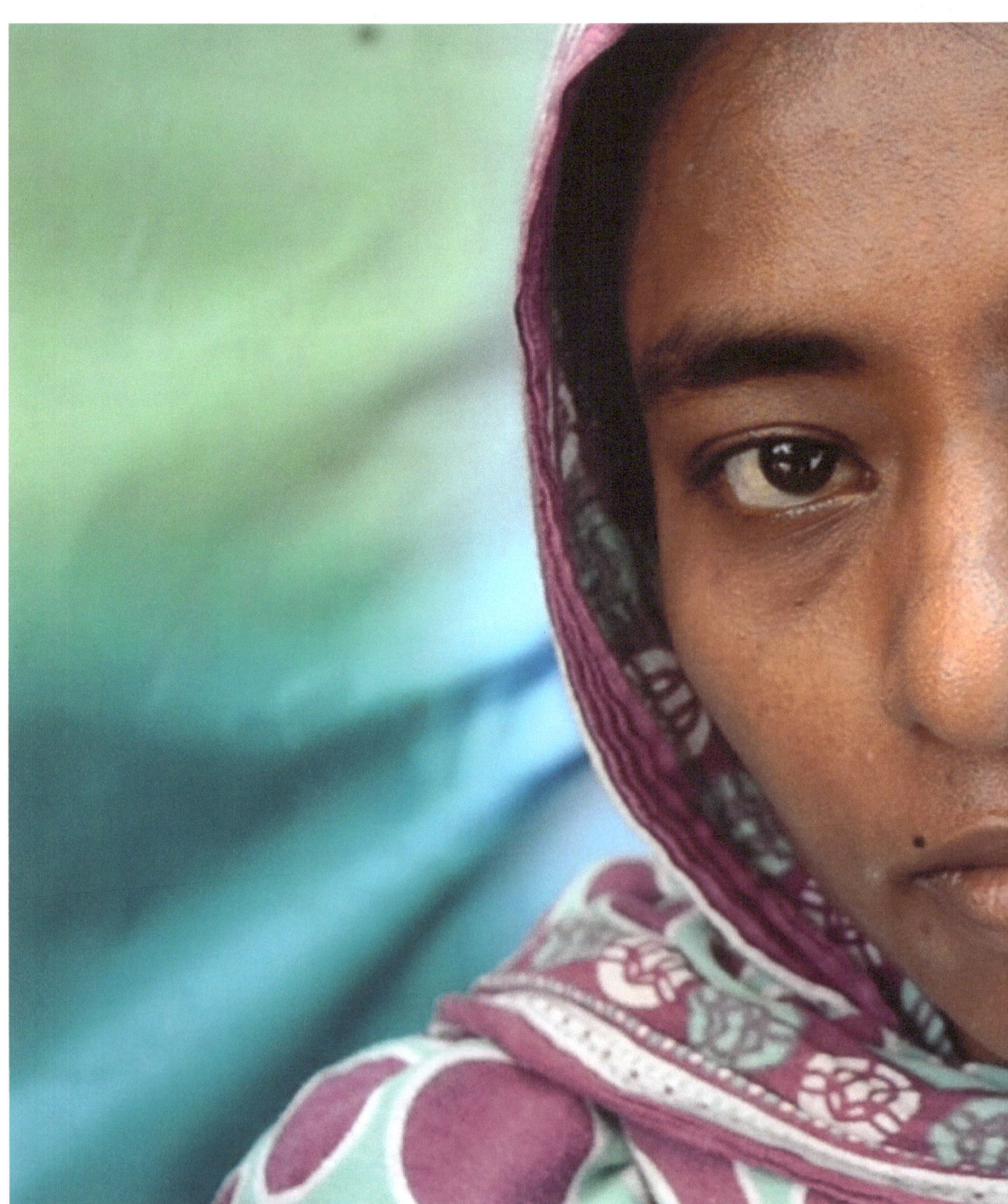

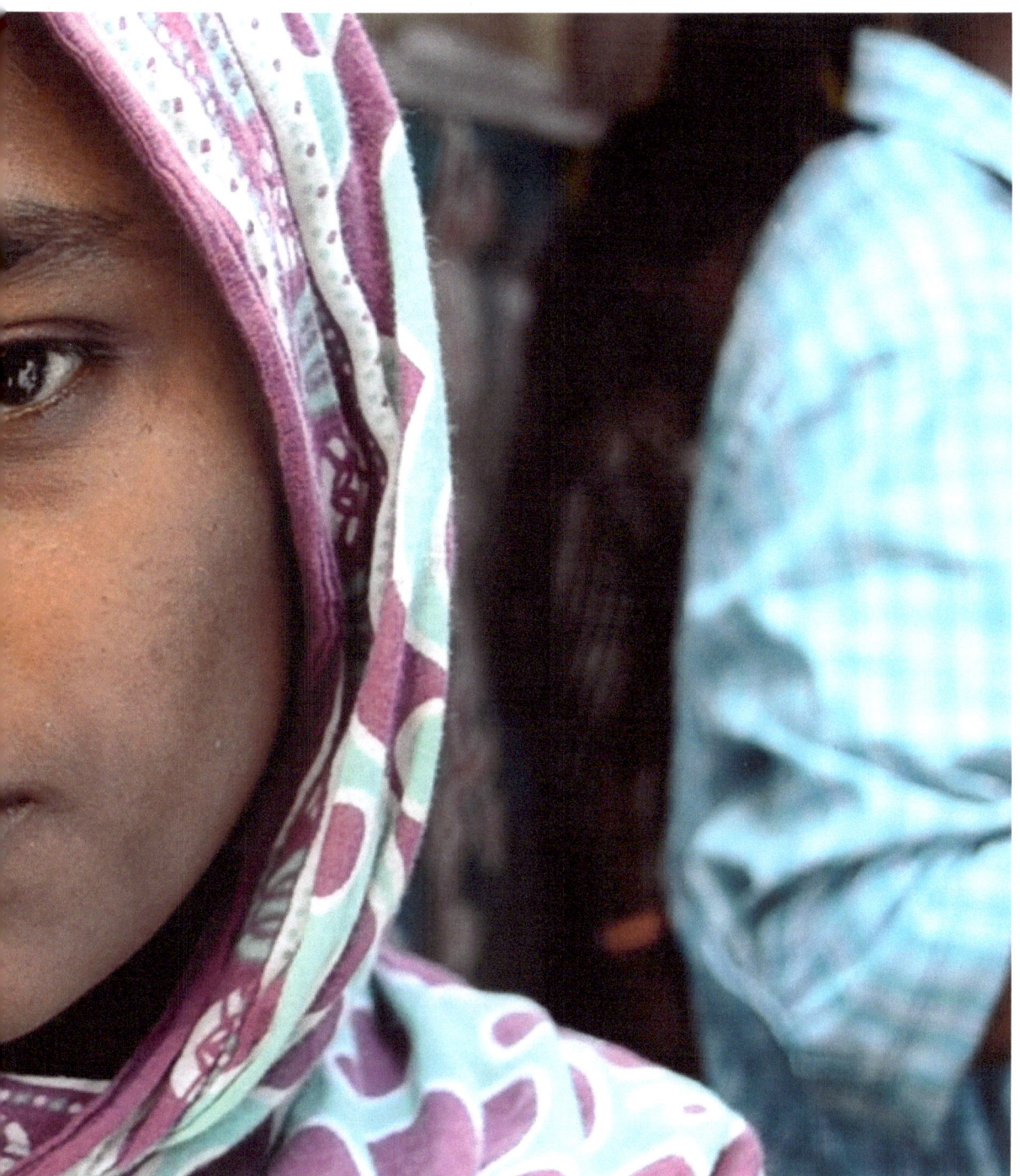

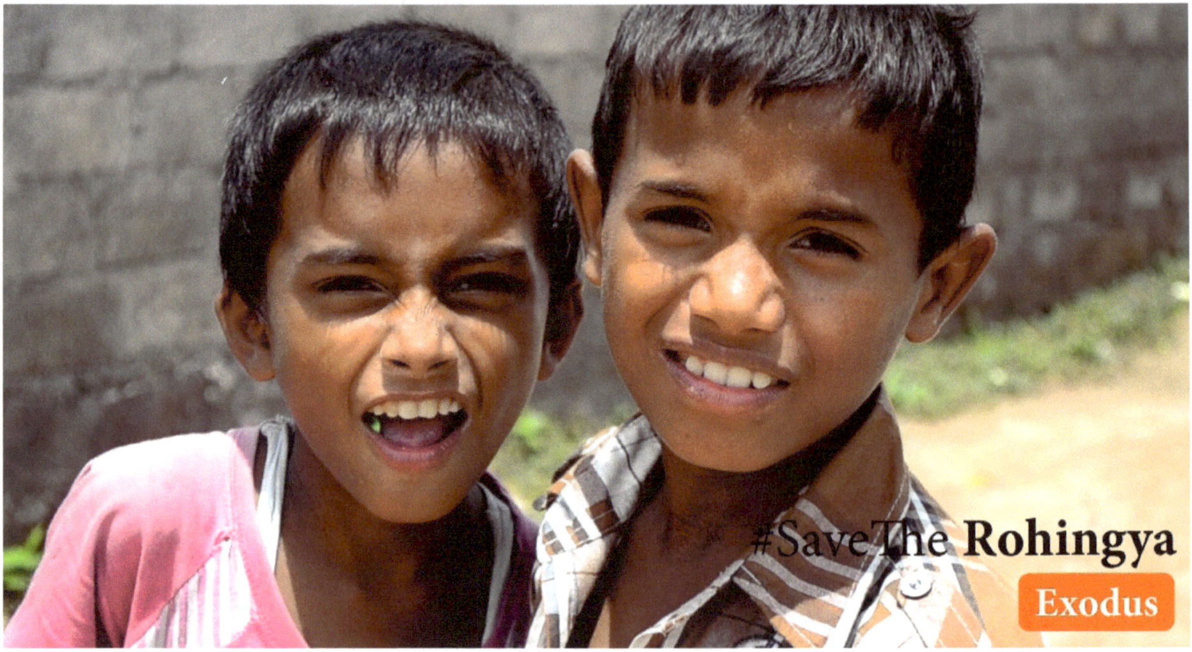

#SaveThe **Rohingya**
Exodus

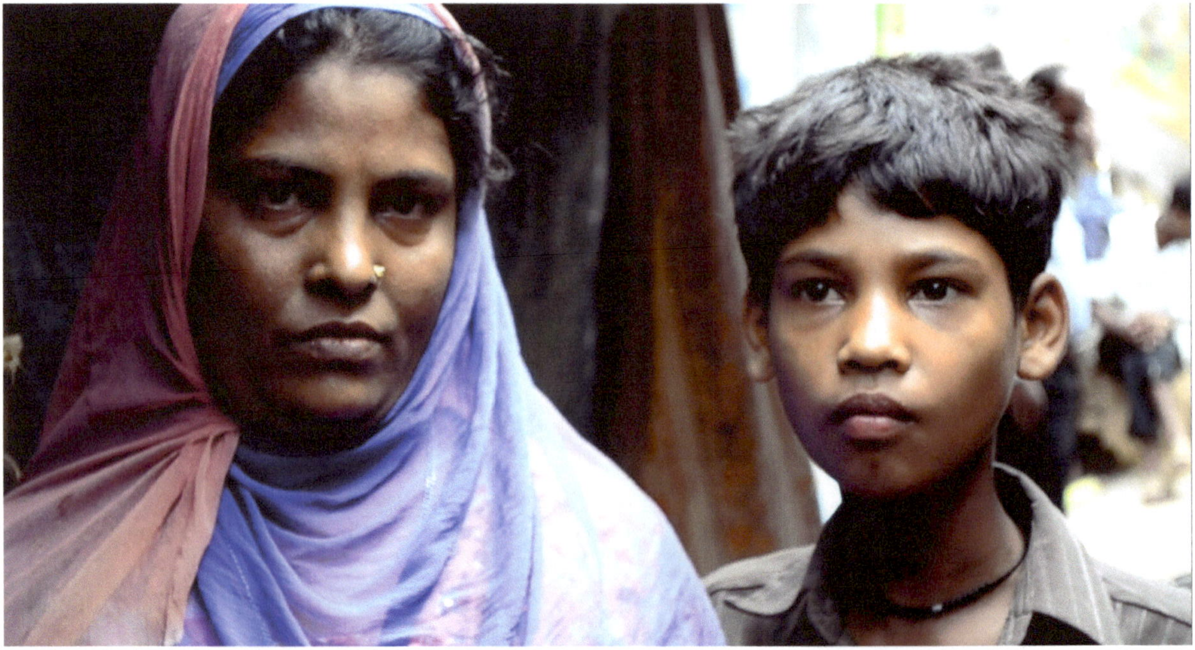

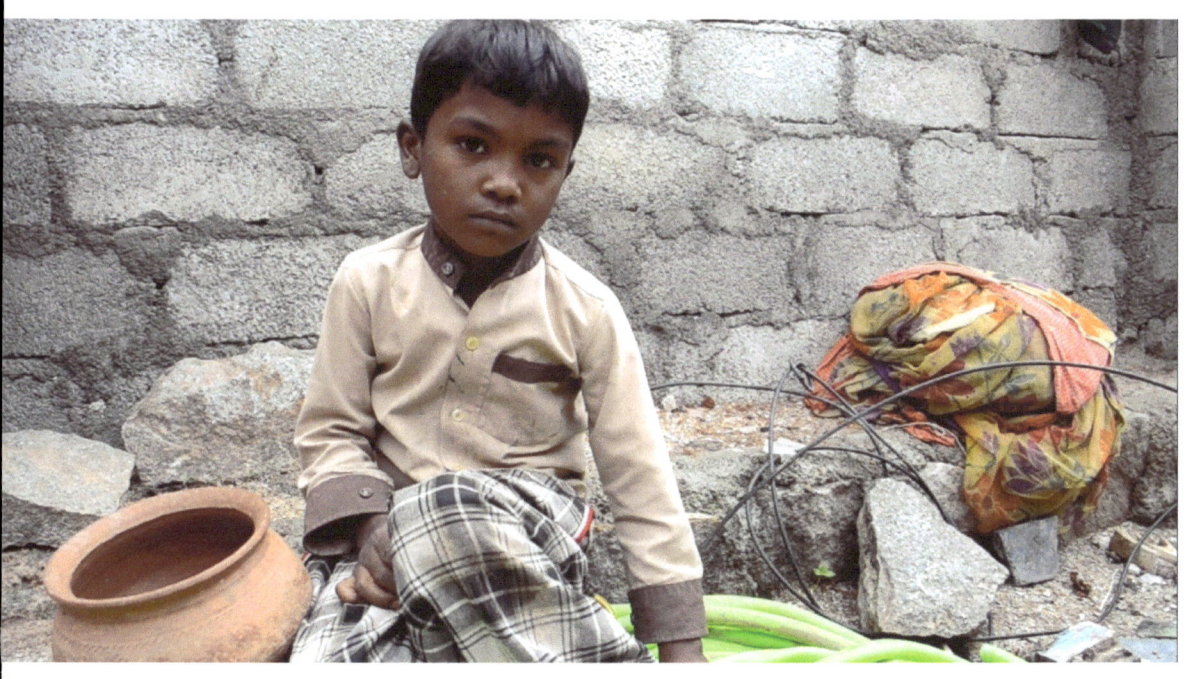
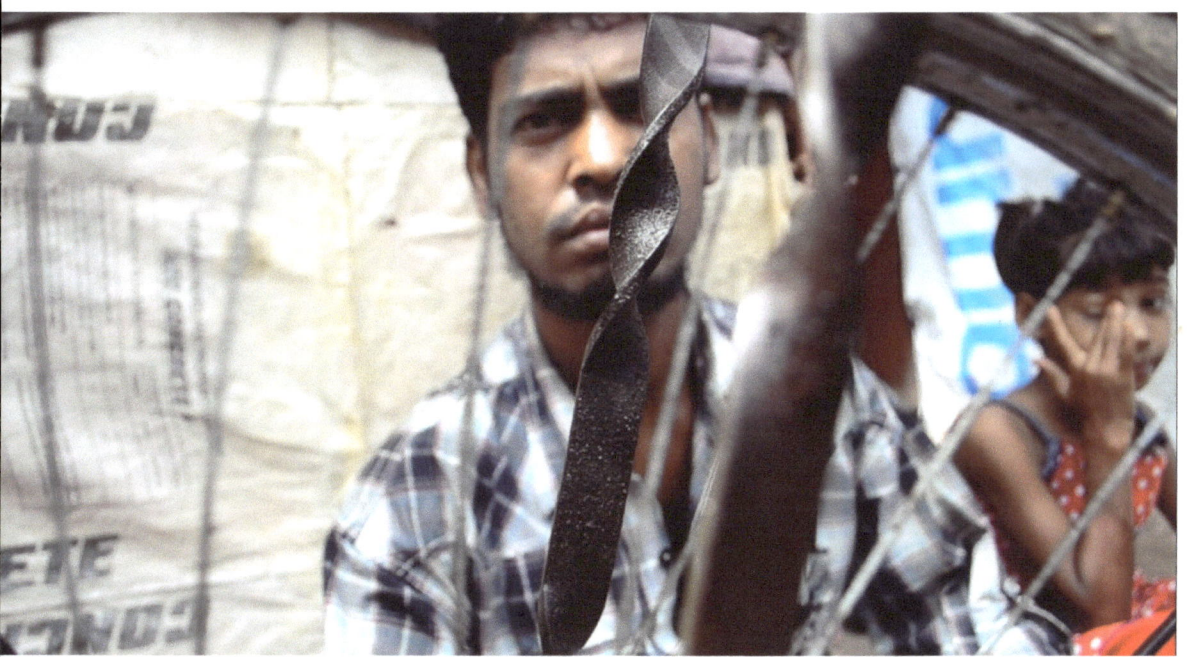

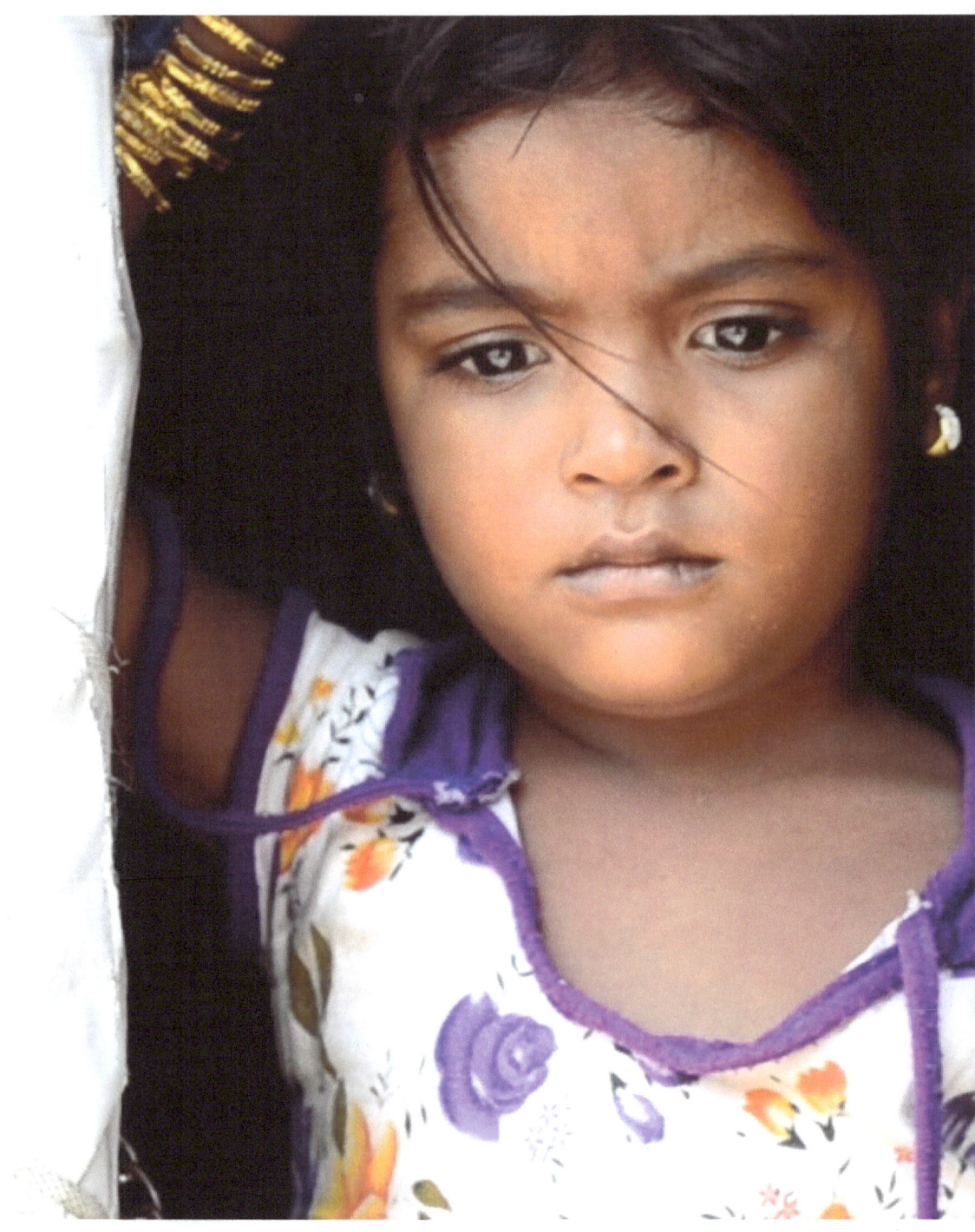

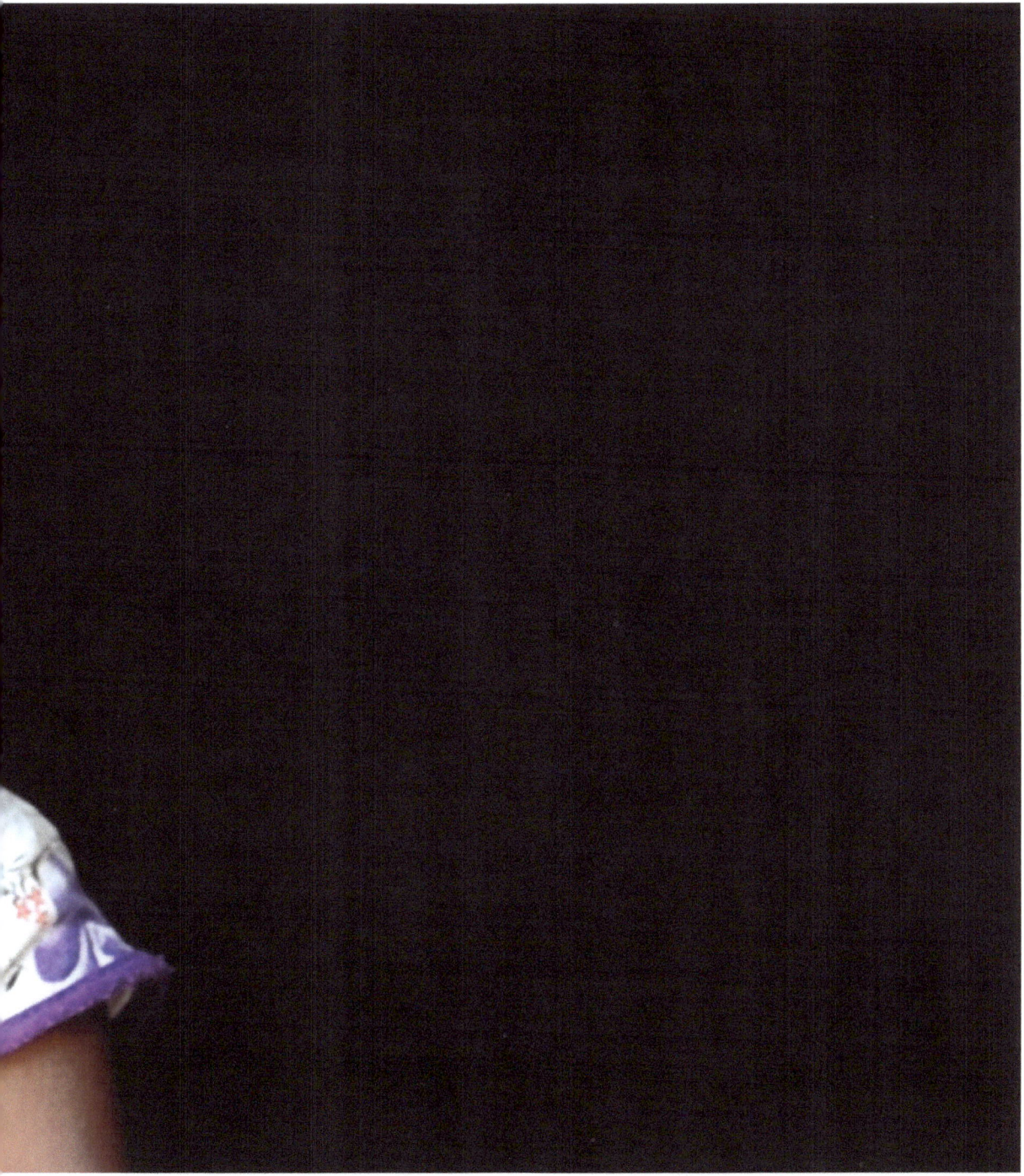

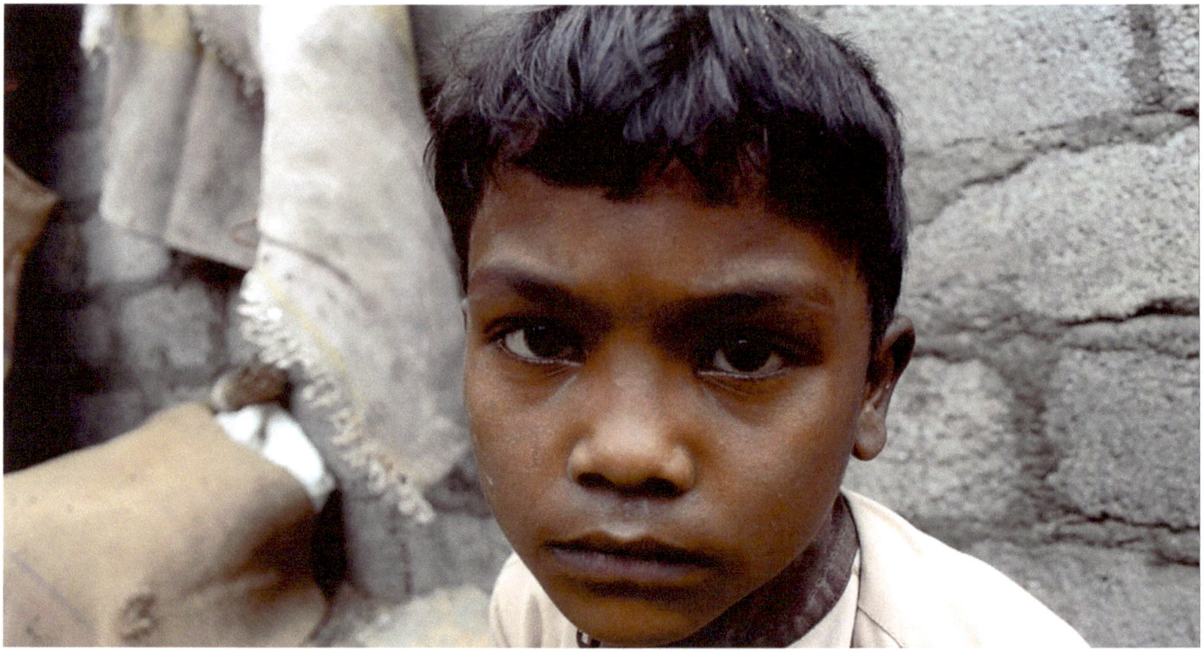

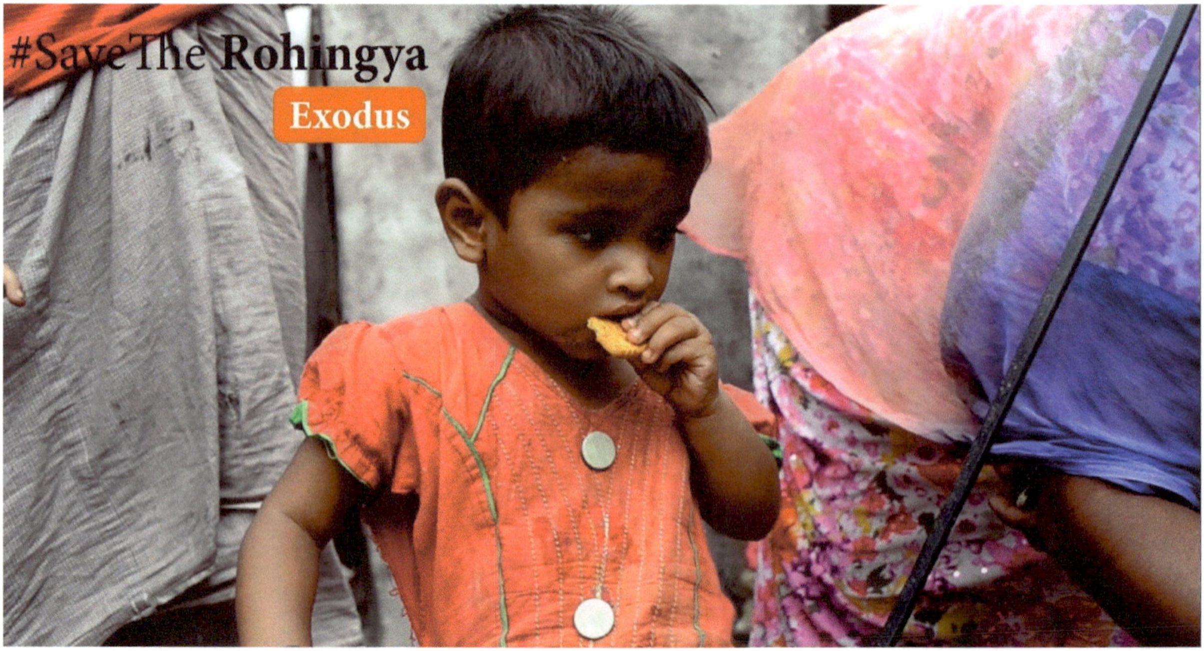

#SaveThe **Rohingya**
Exodus

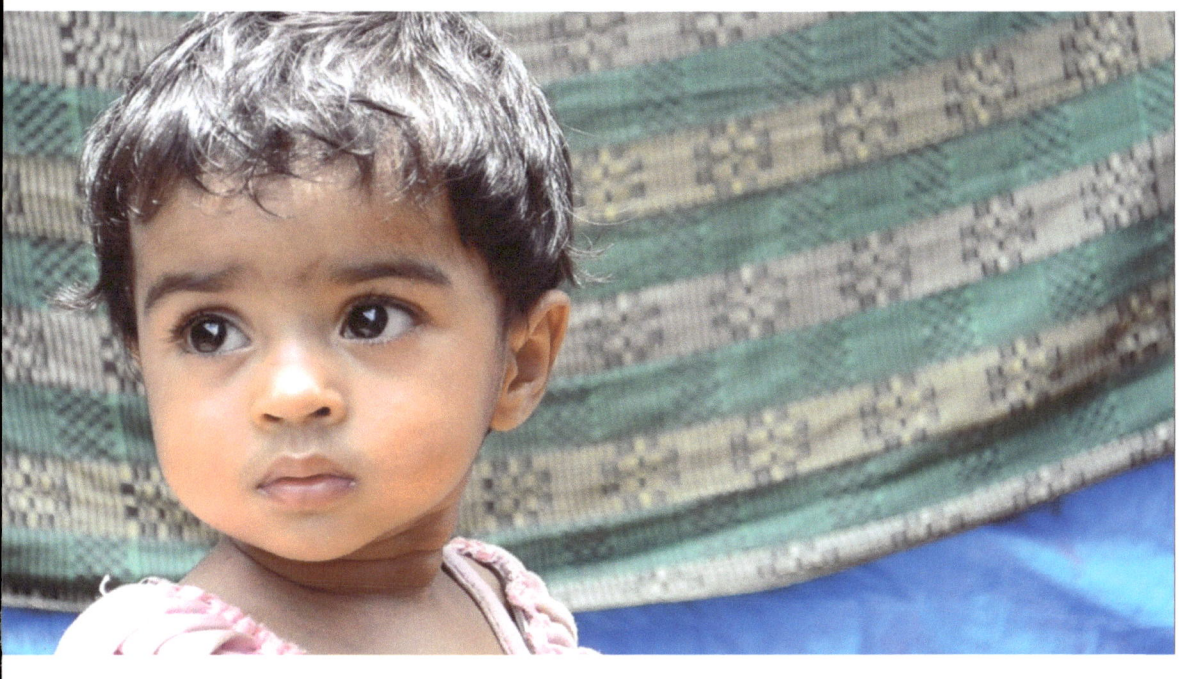
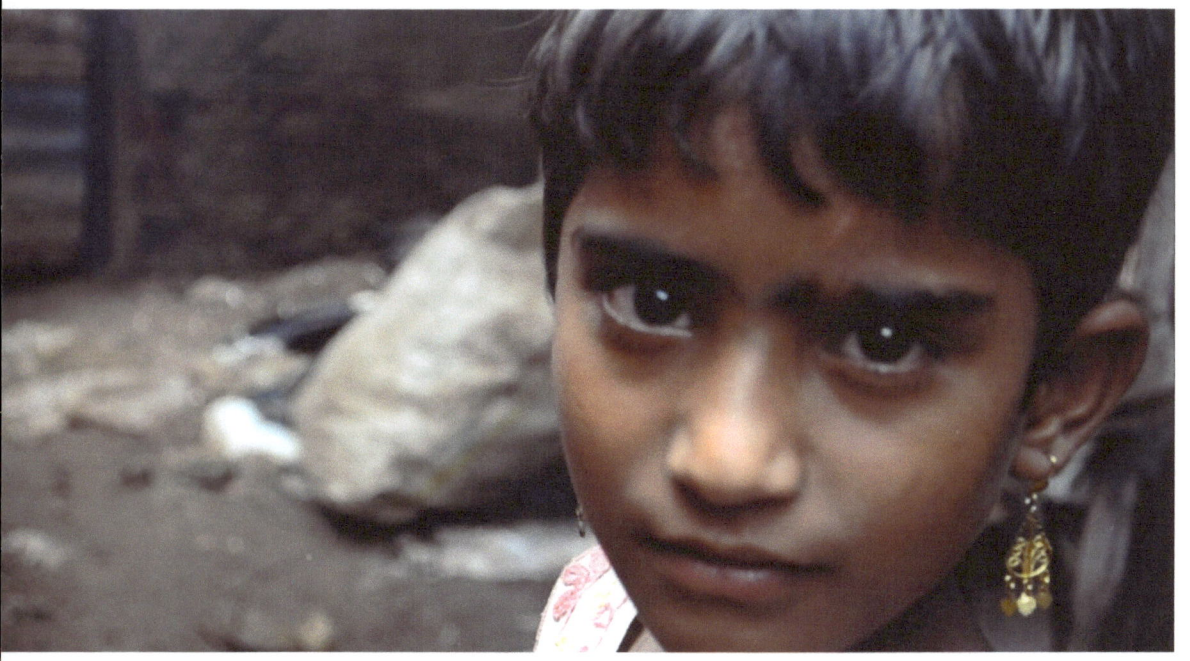

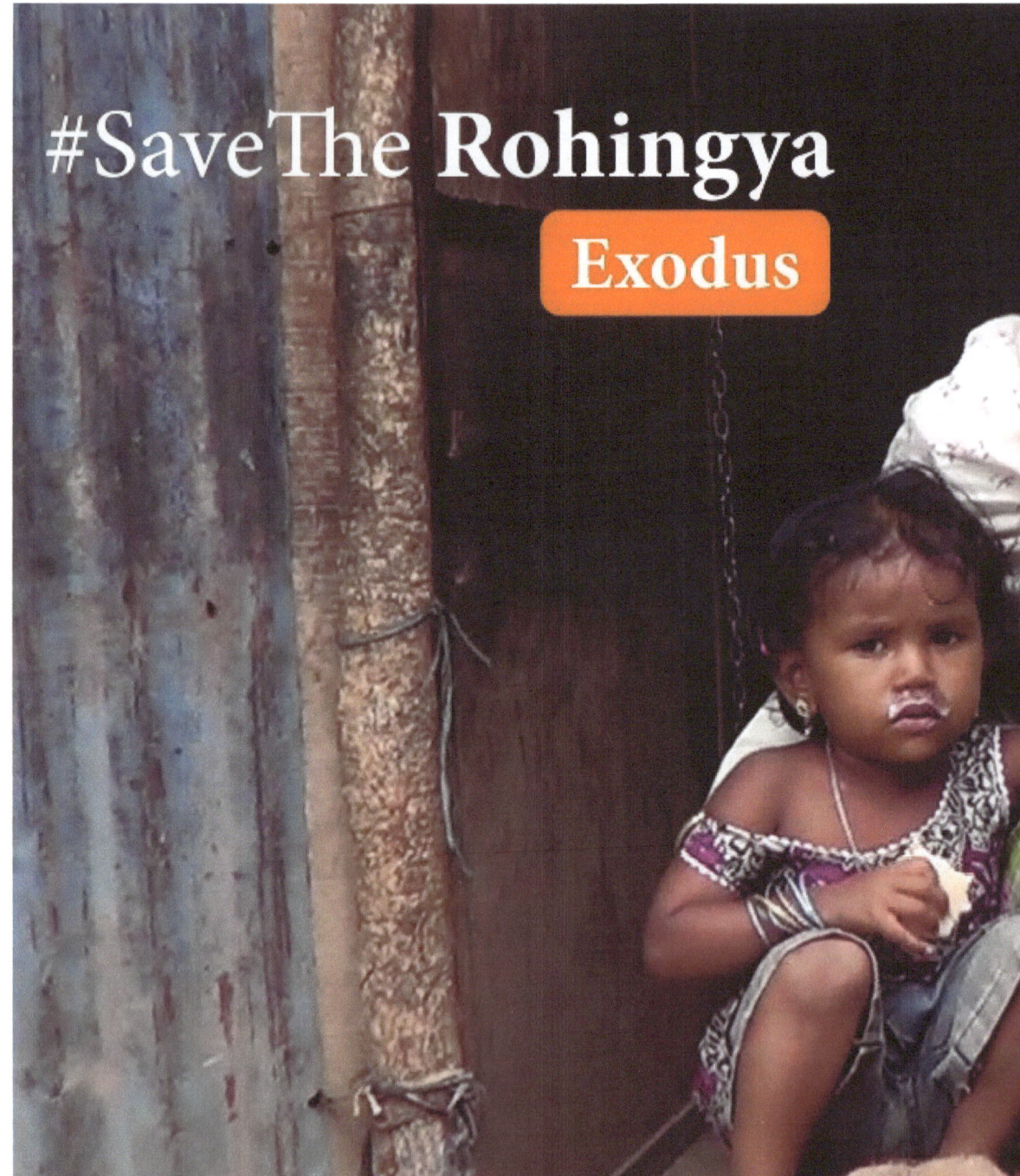

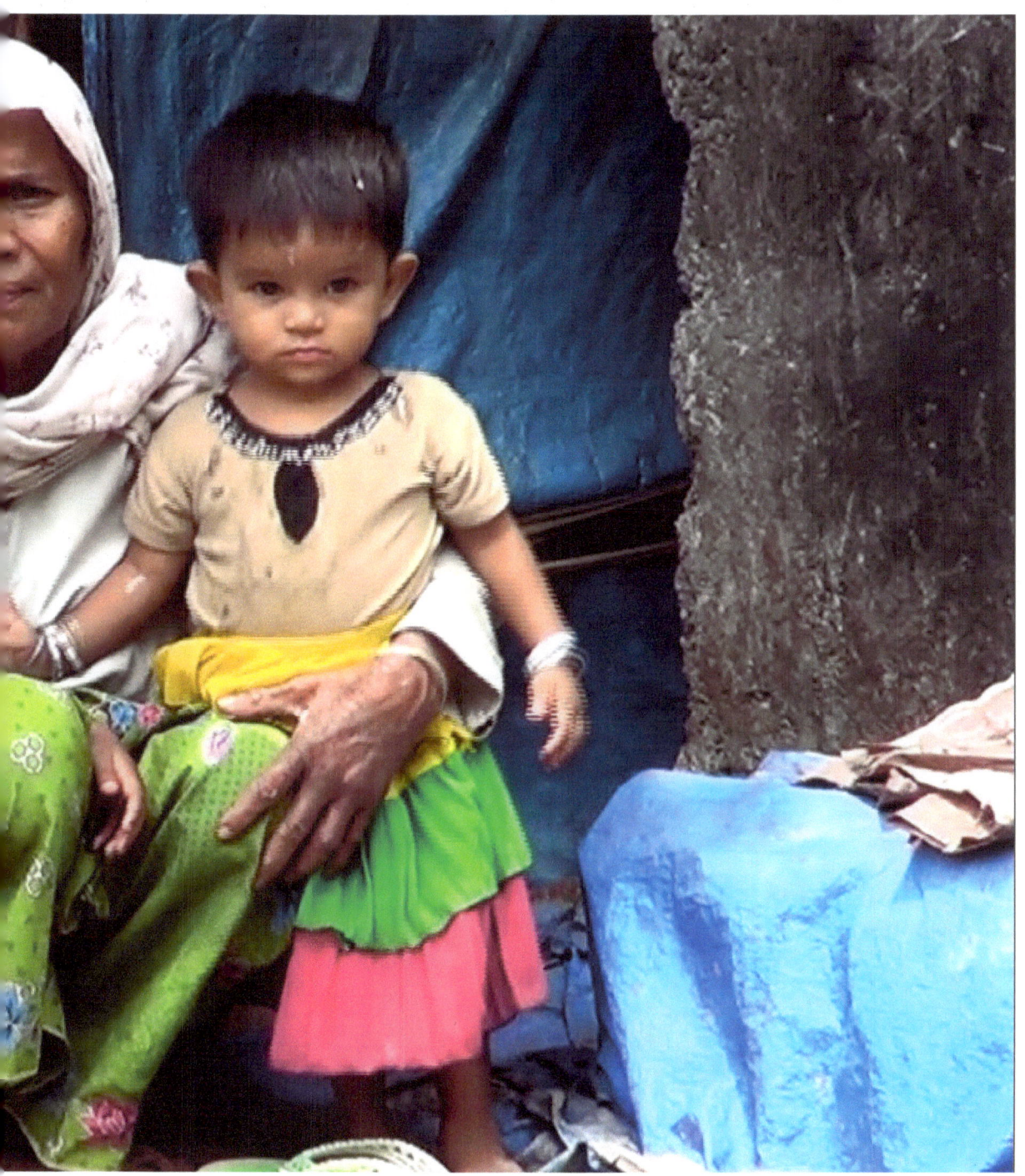

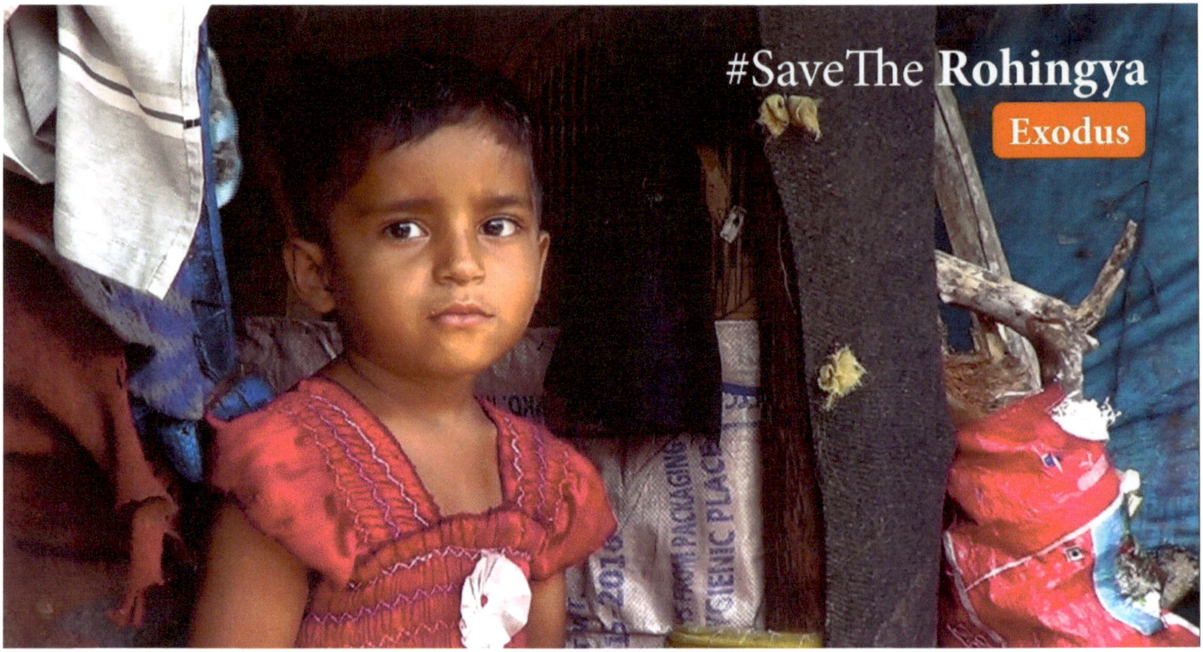

#SaveThe Rohingya
Exodus

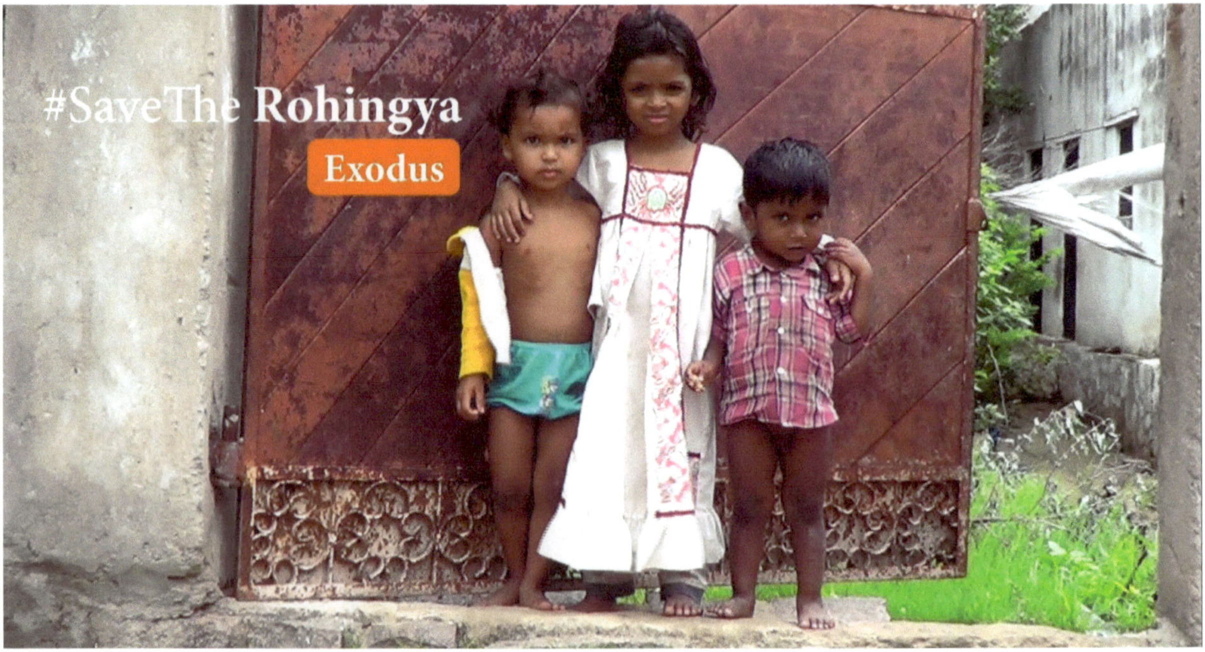

#SaveThe Rohingya
Exodus

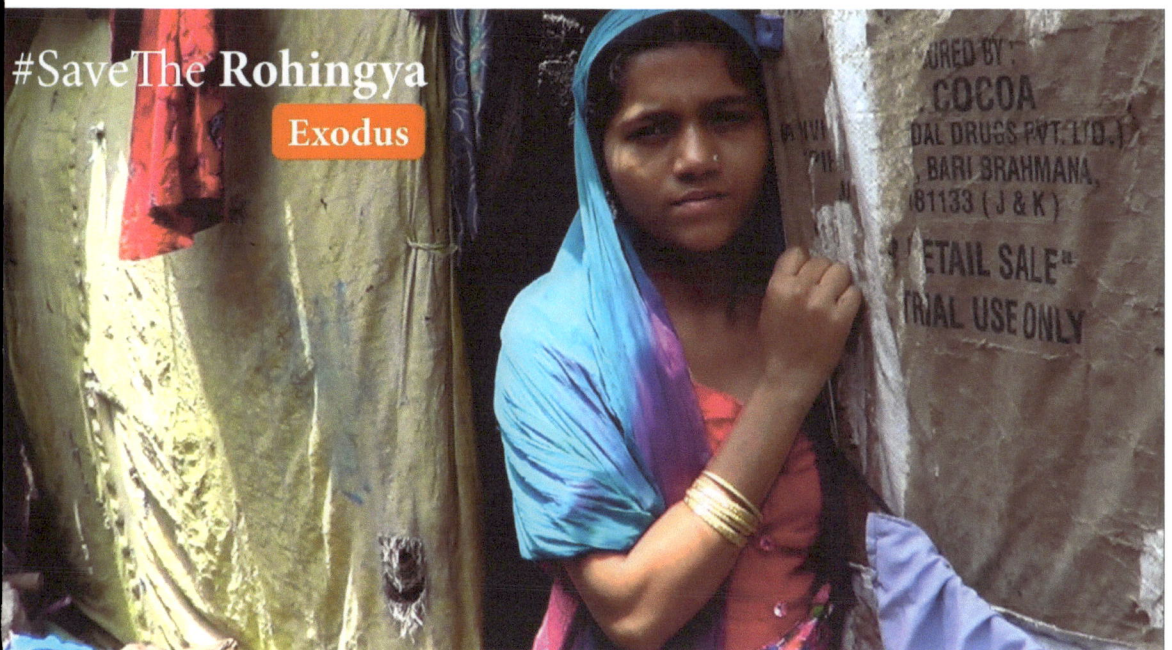
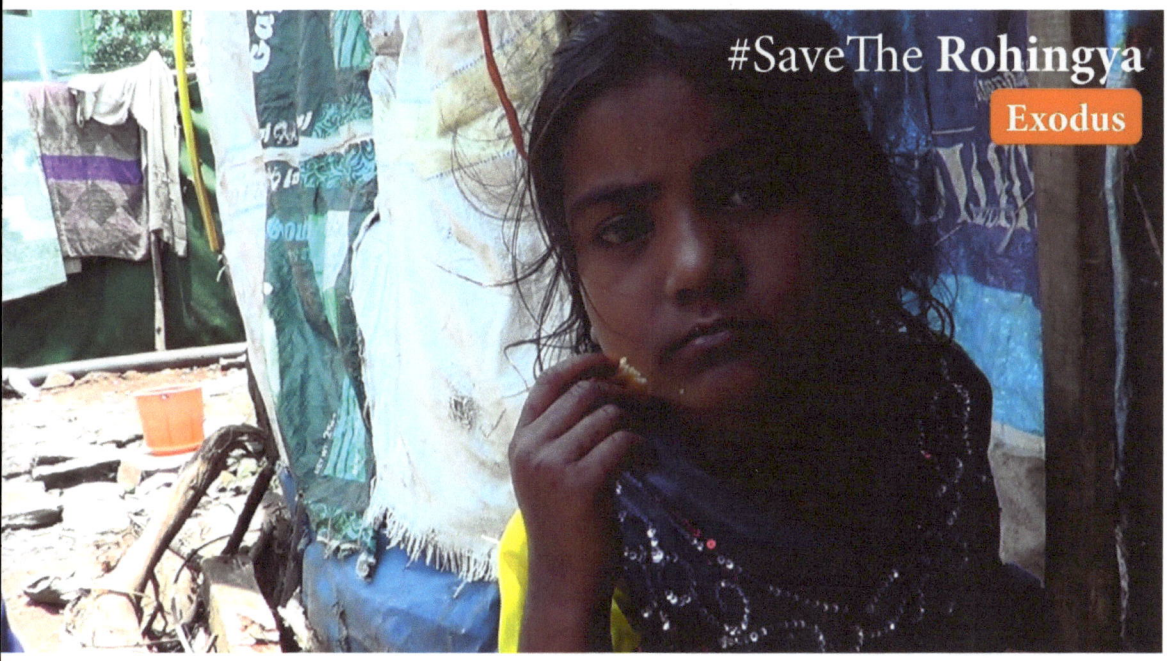

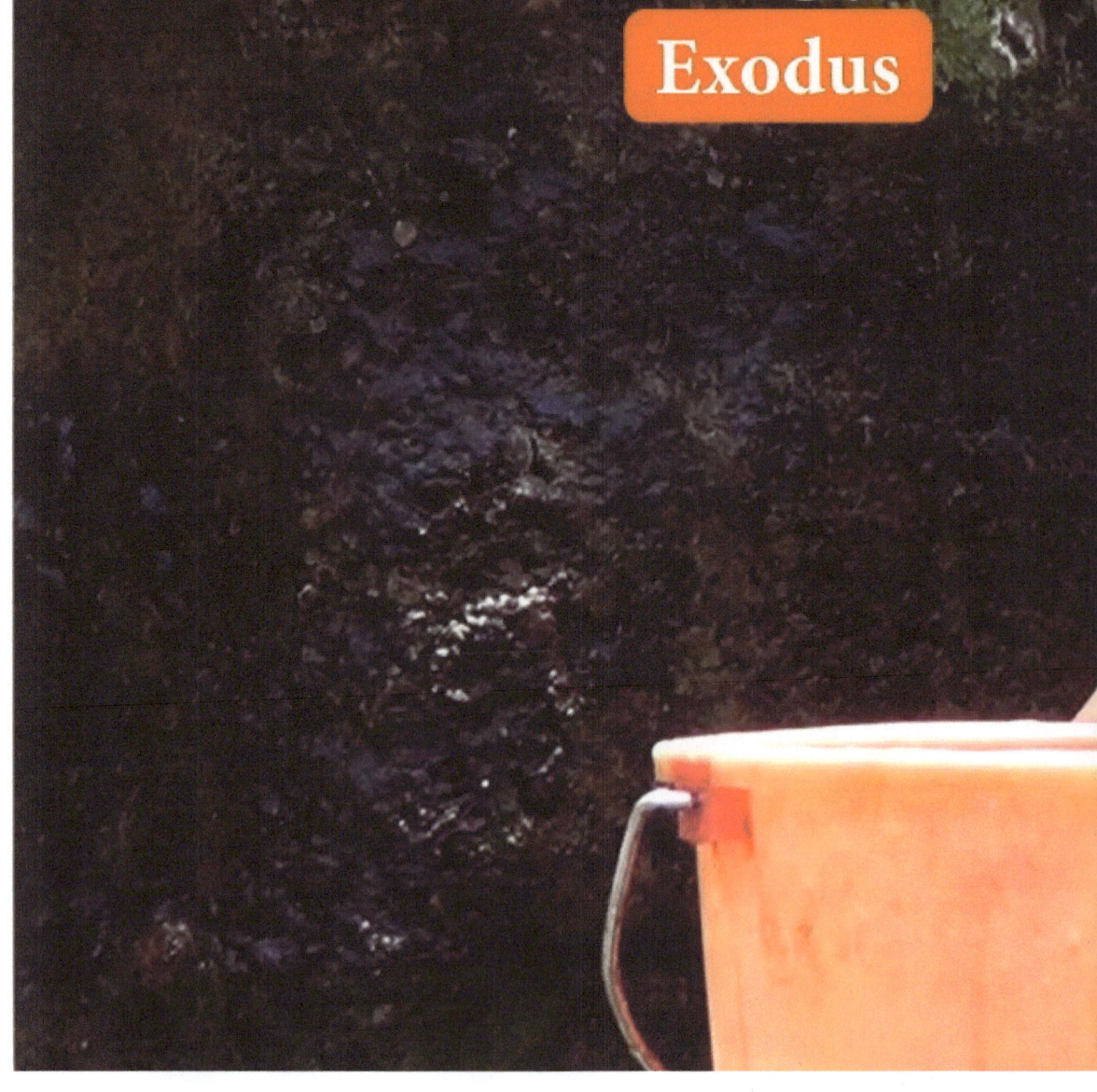

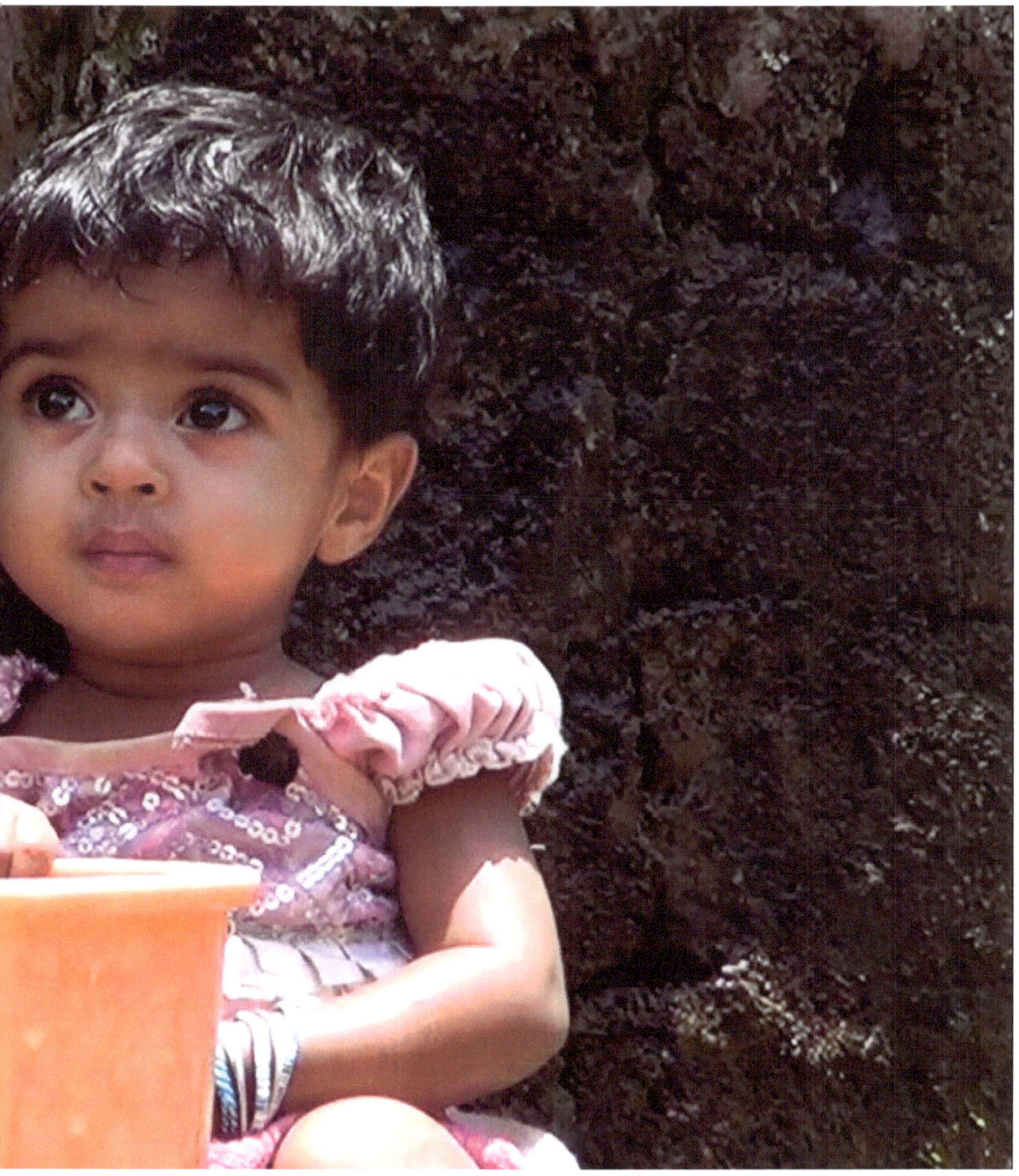

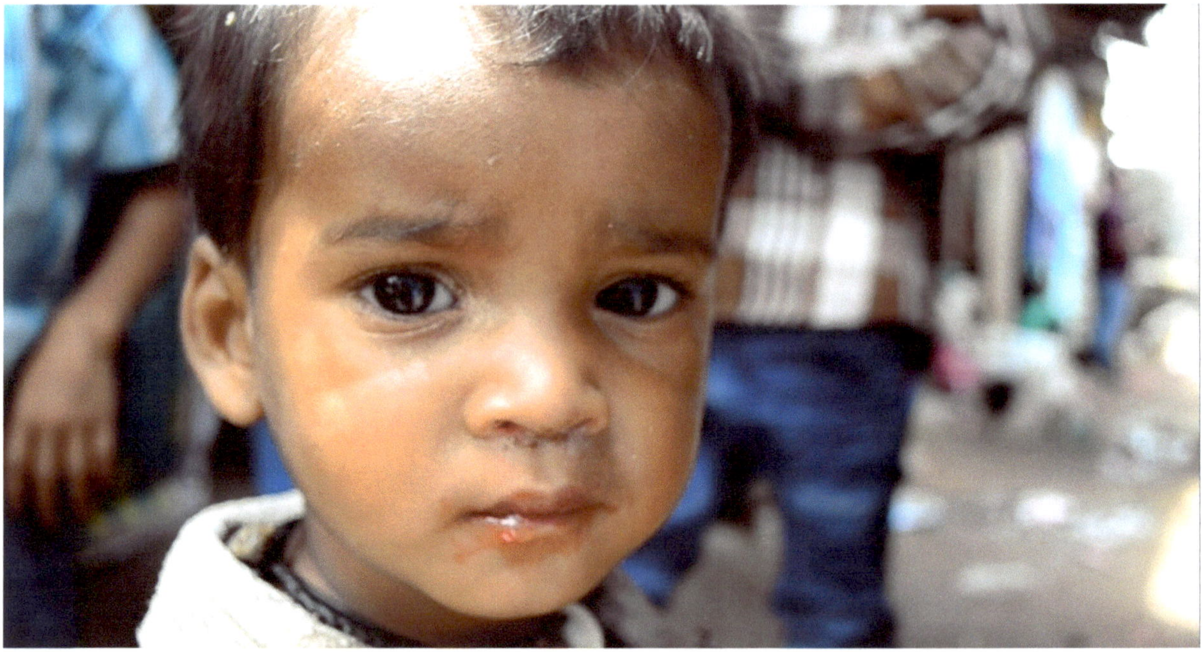

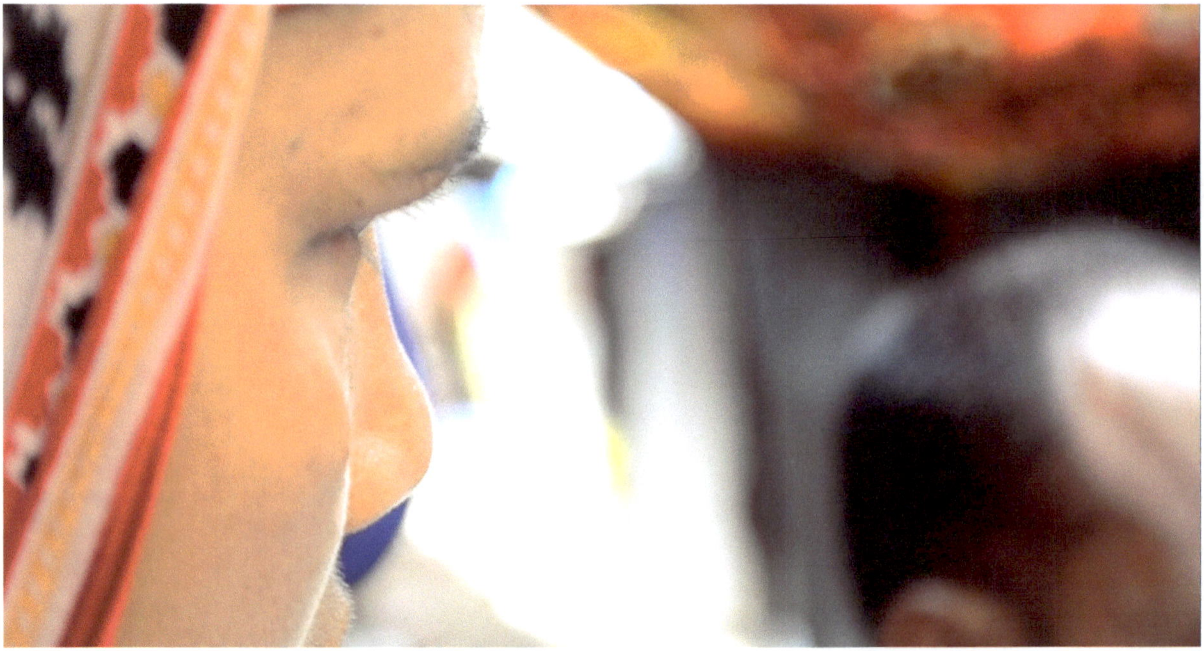

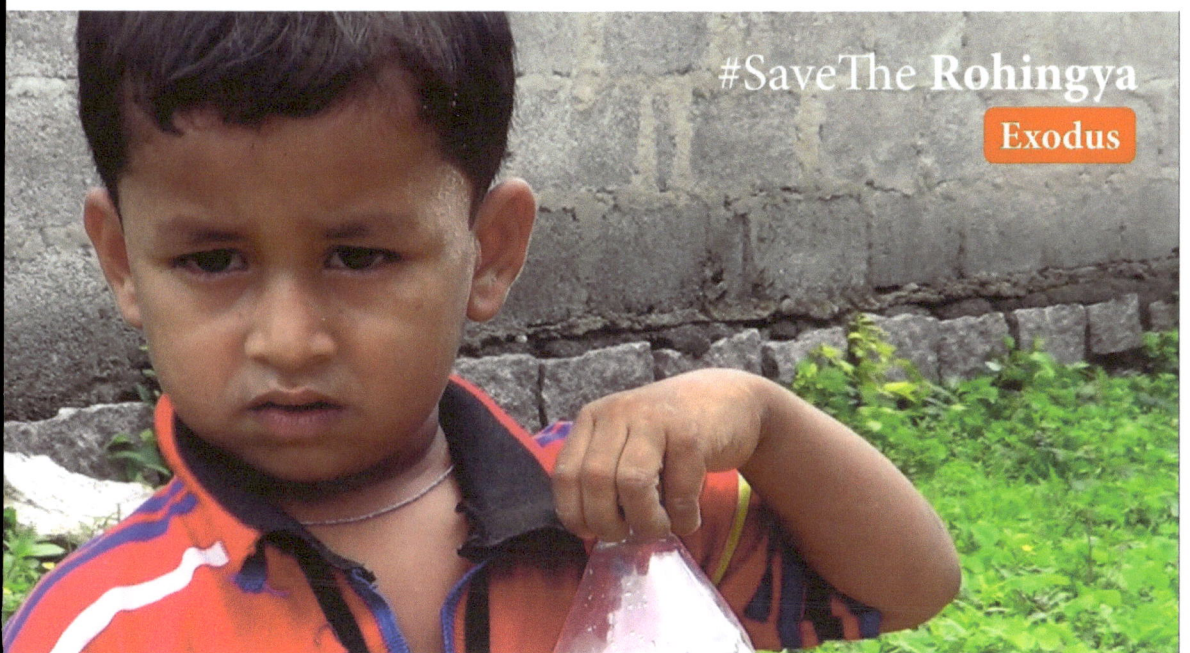

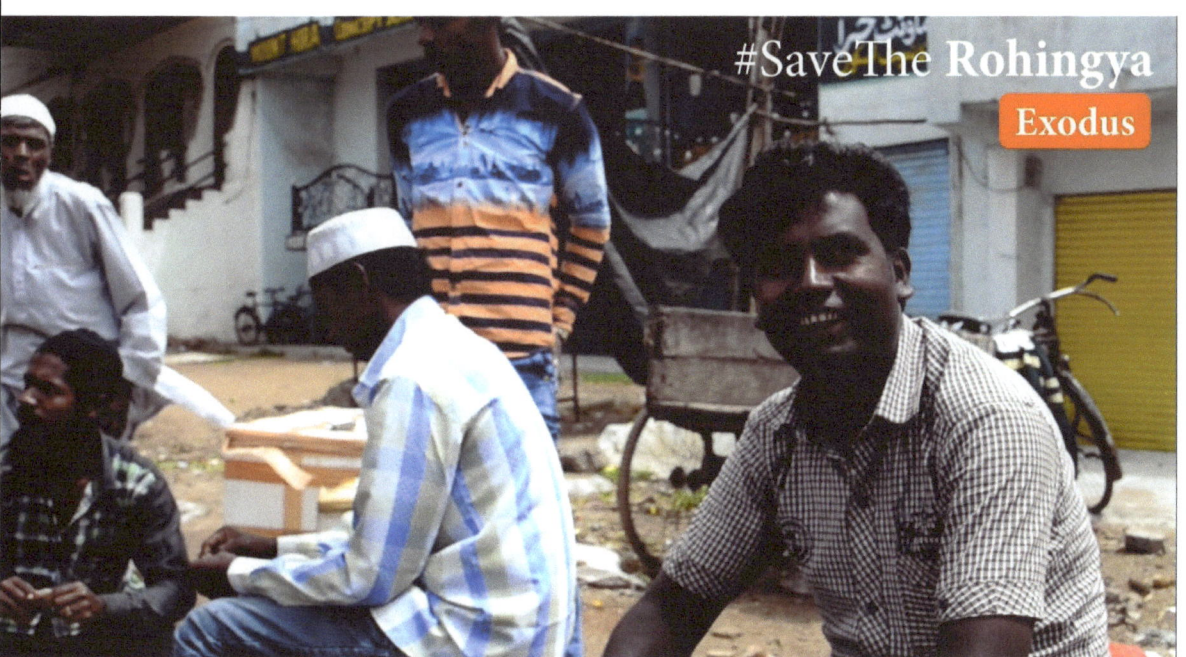

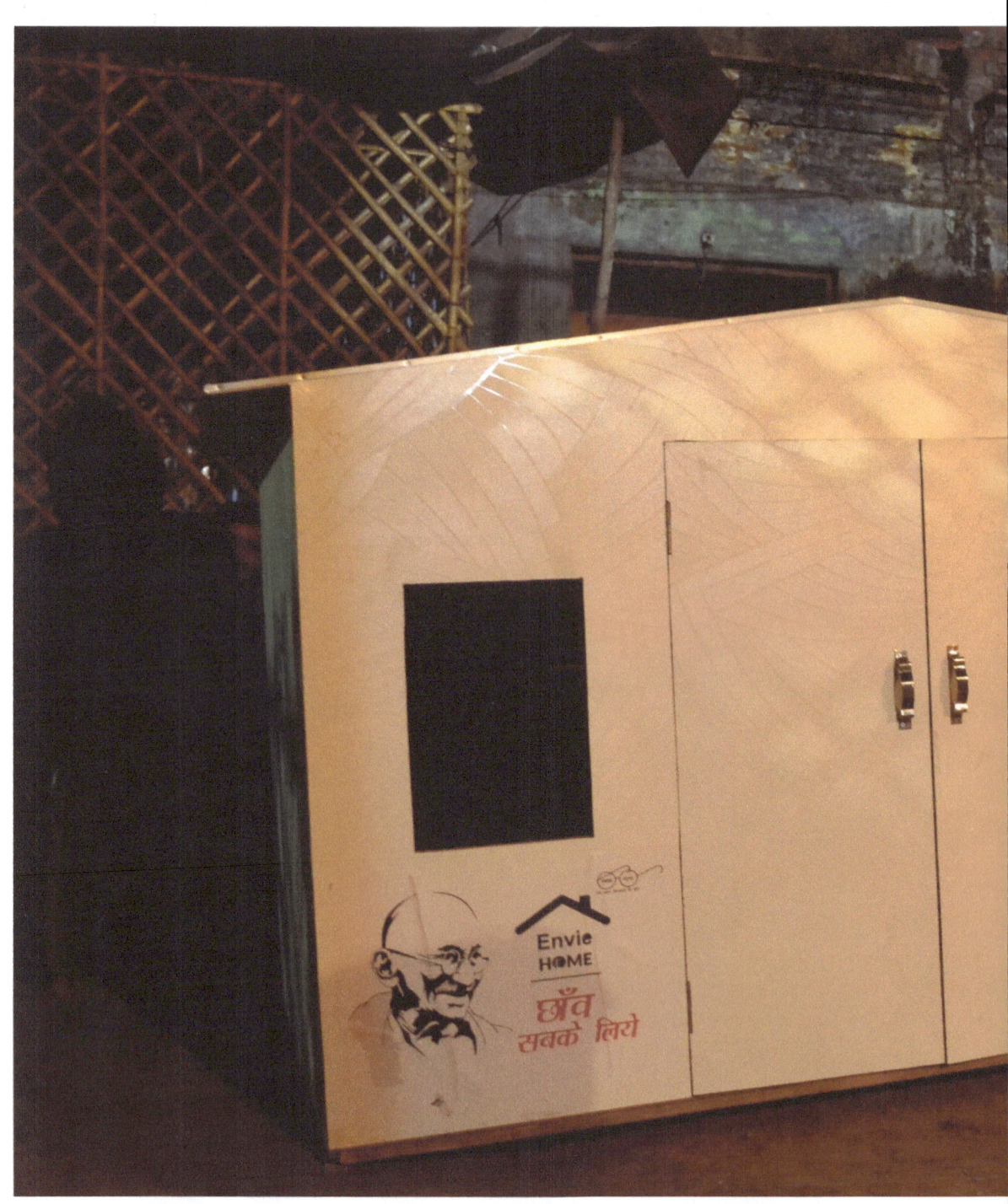

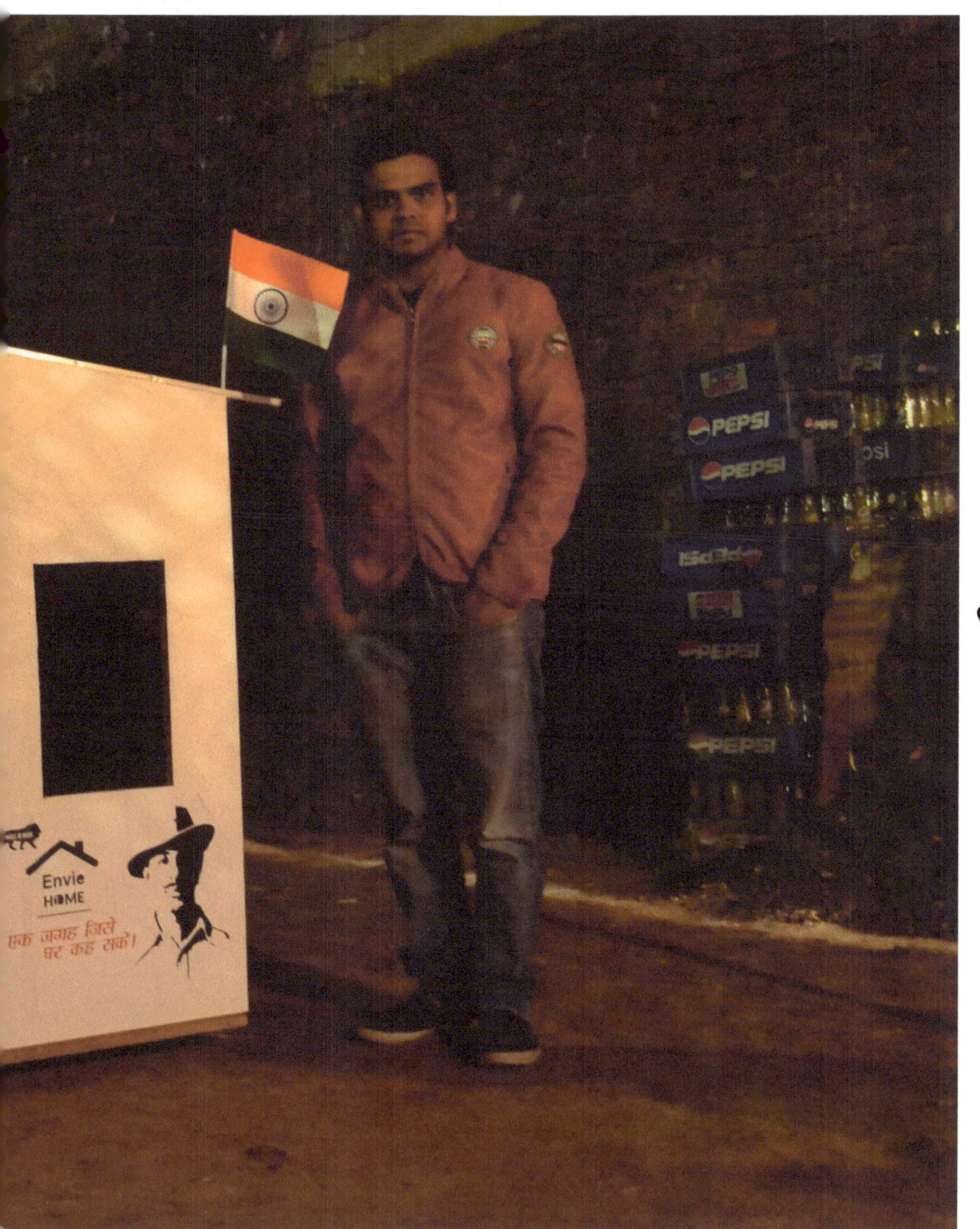

Envie Home for Homeless

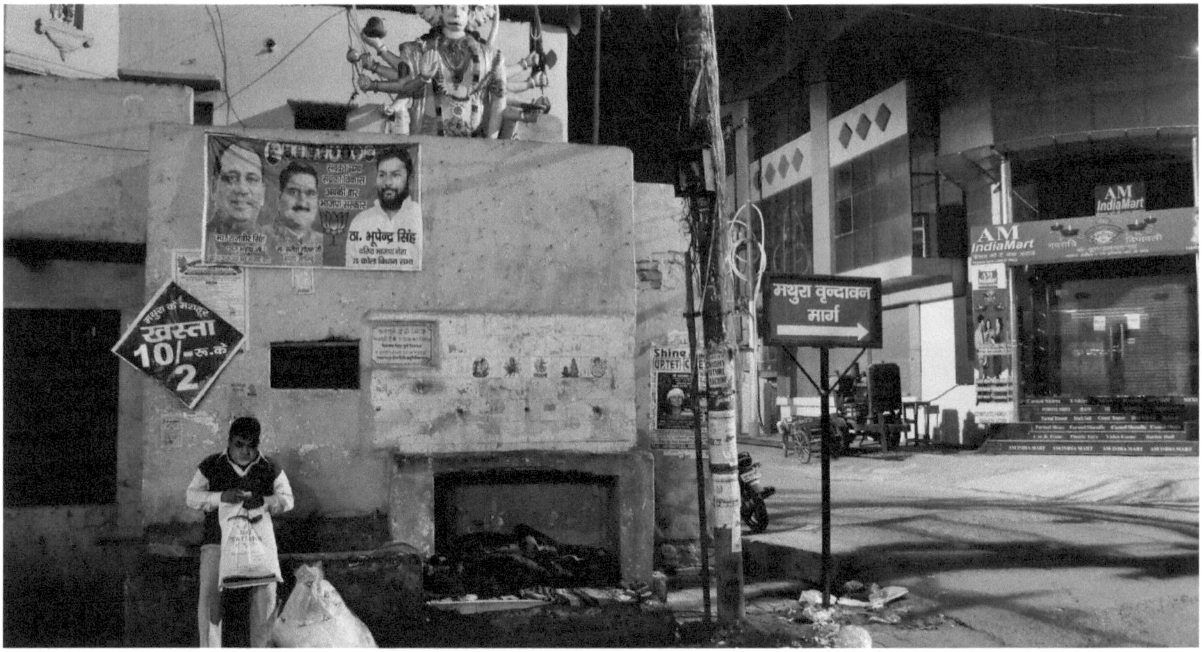

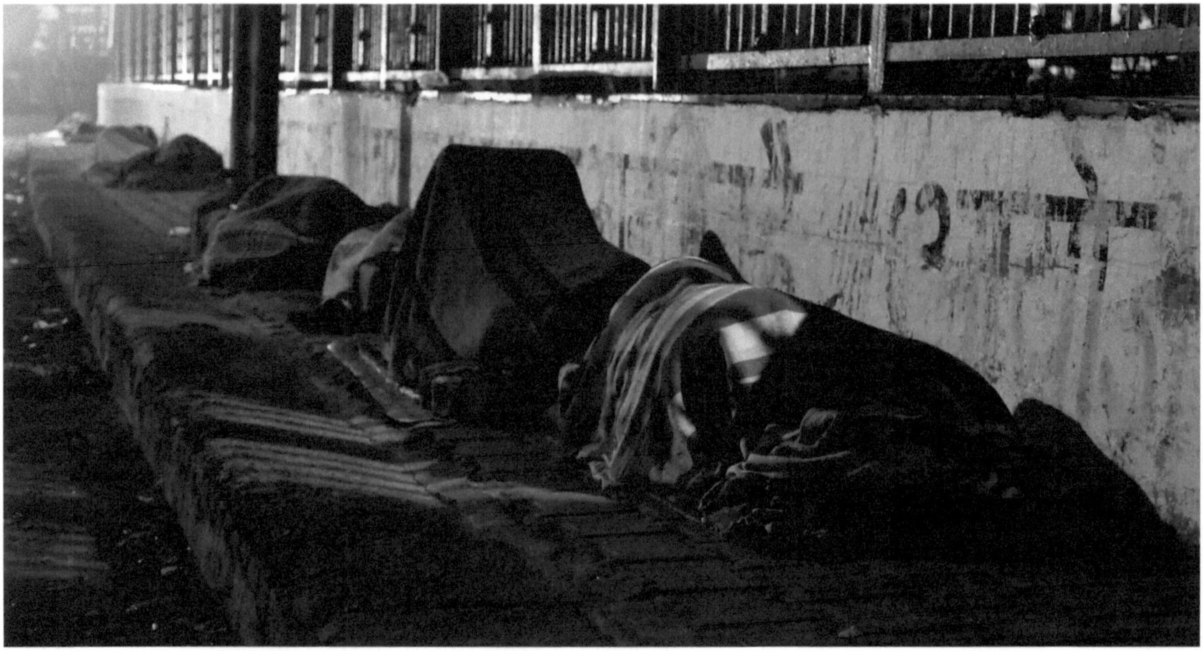

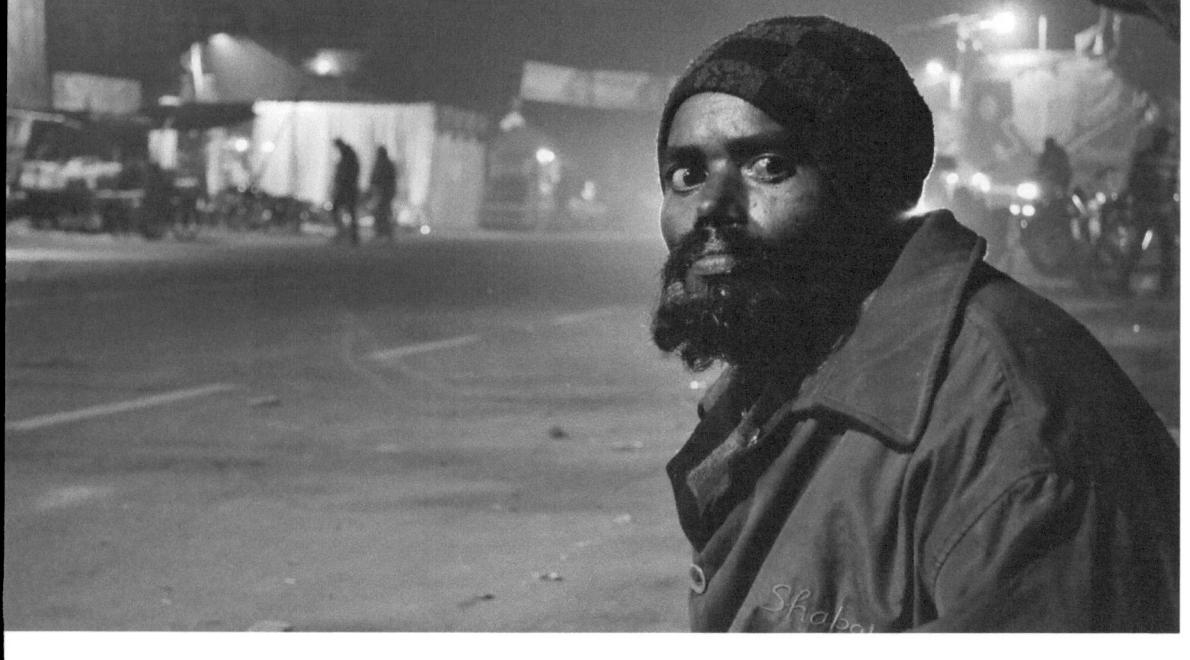
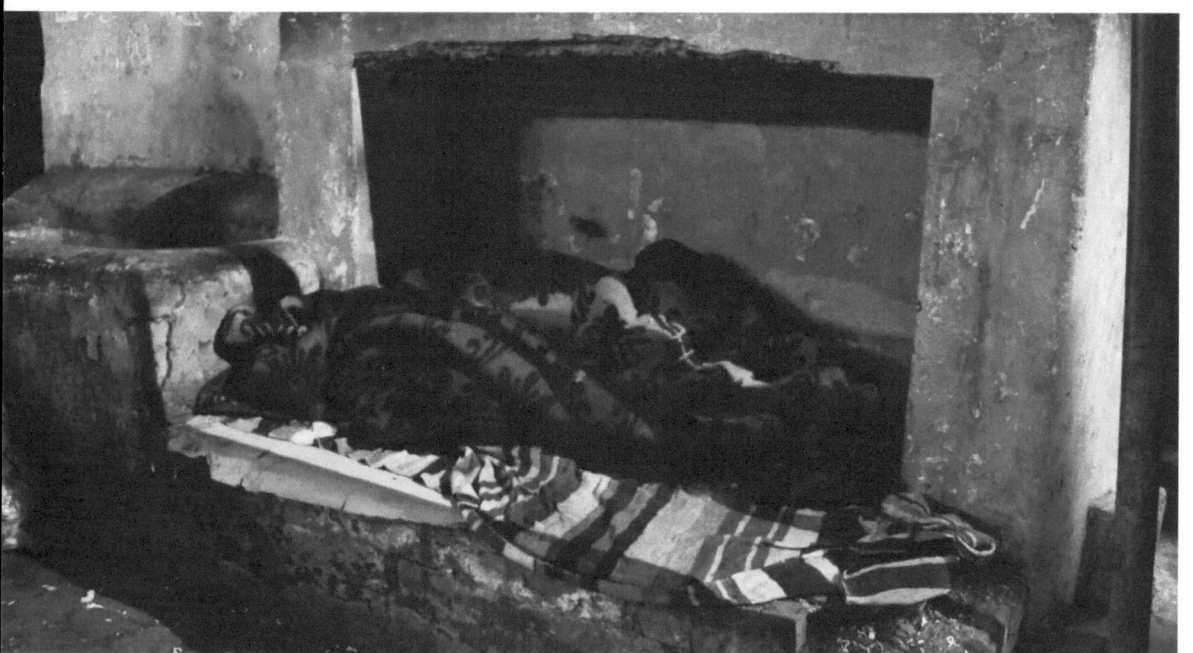

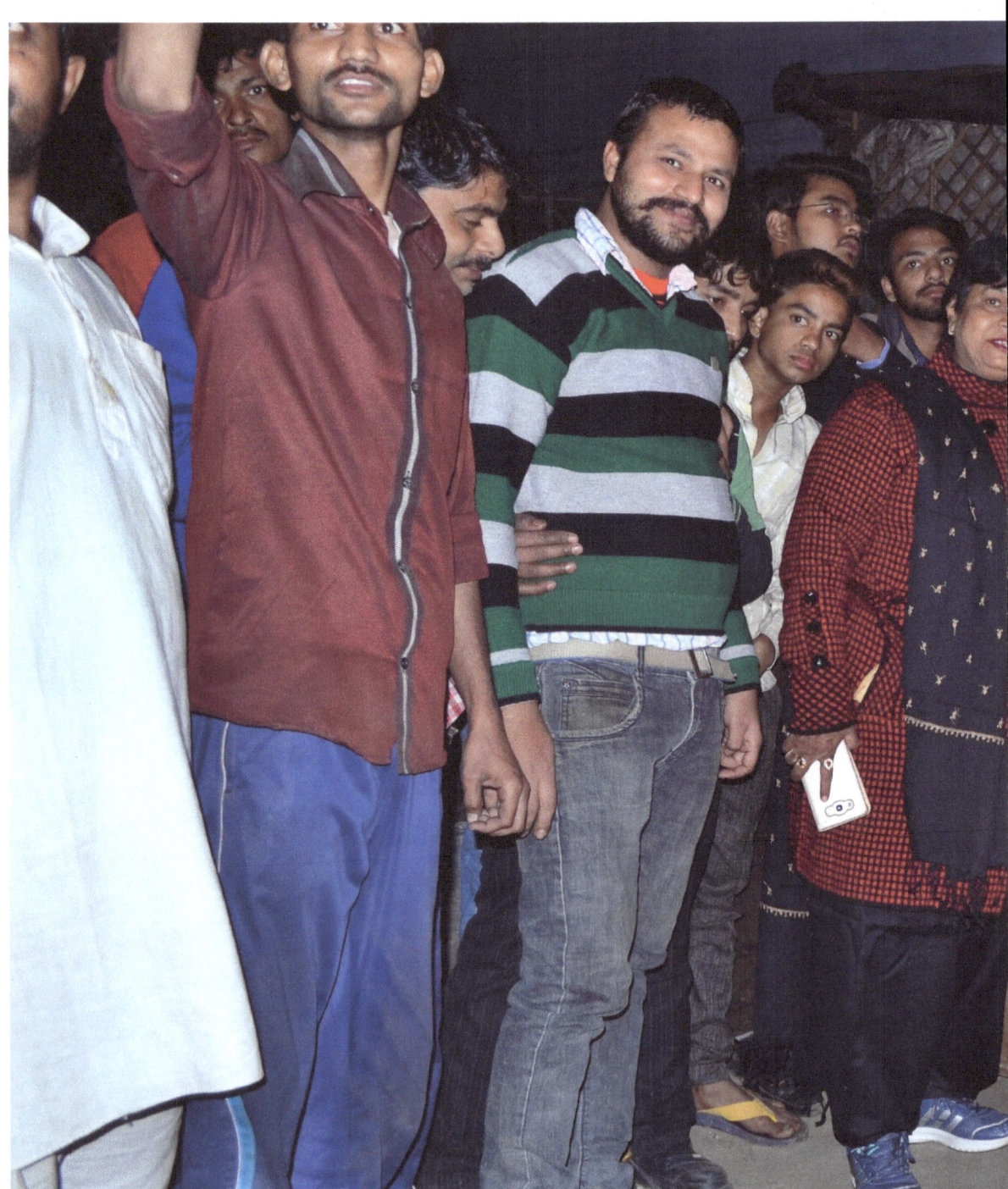

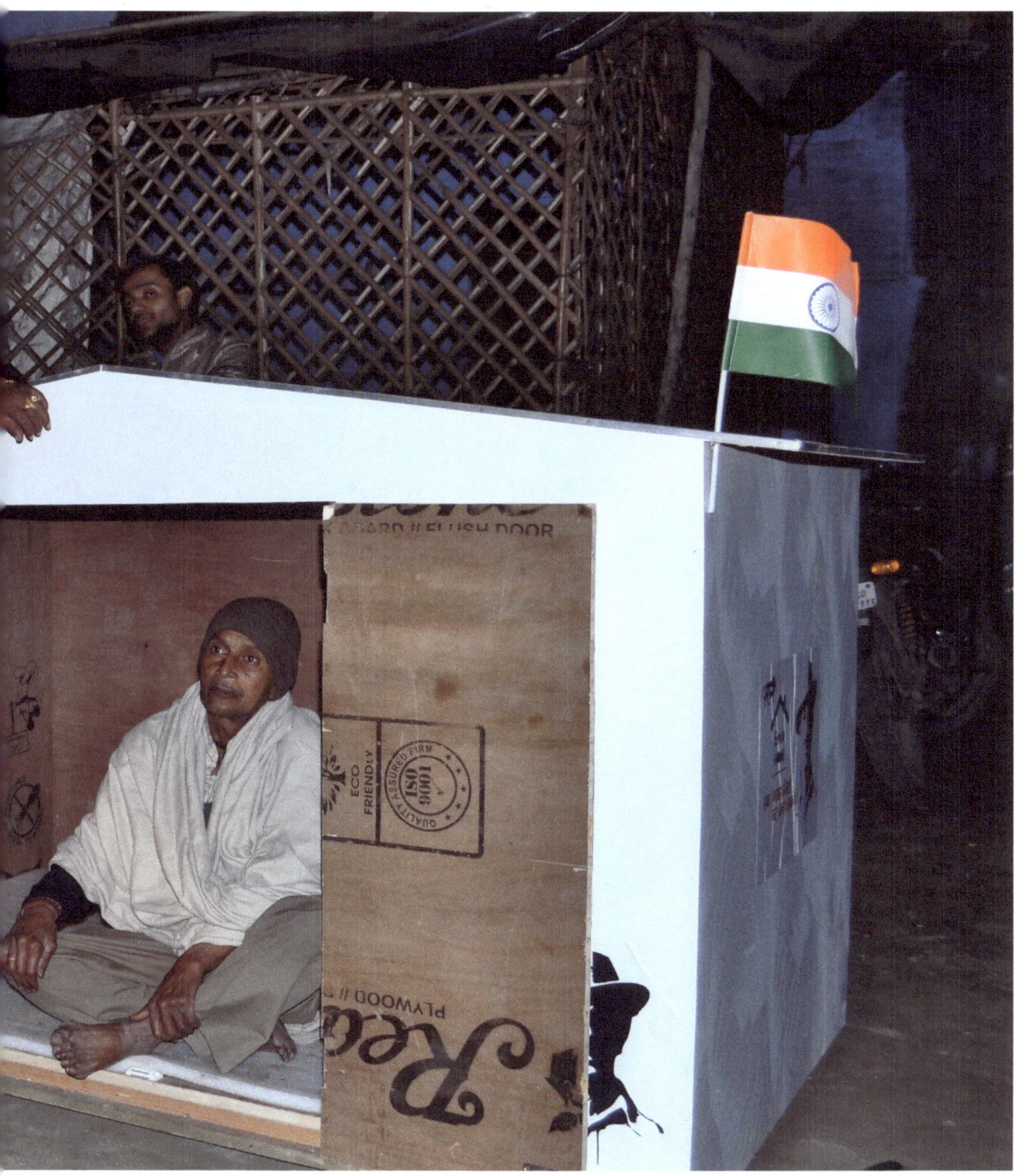

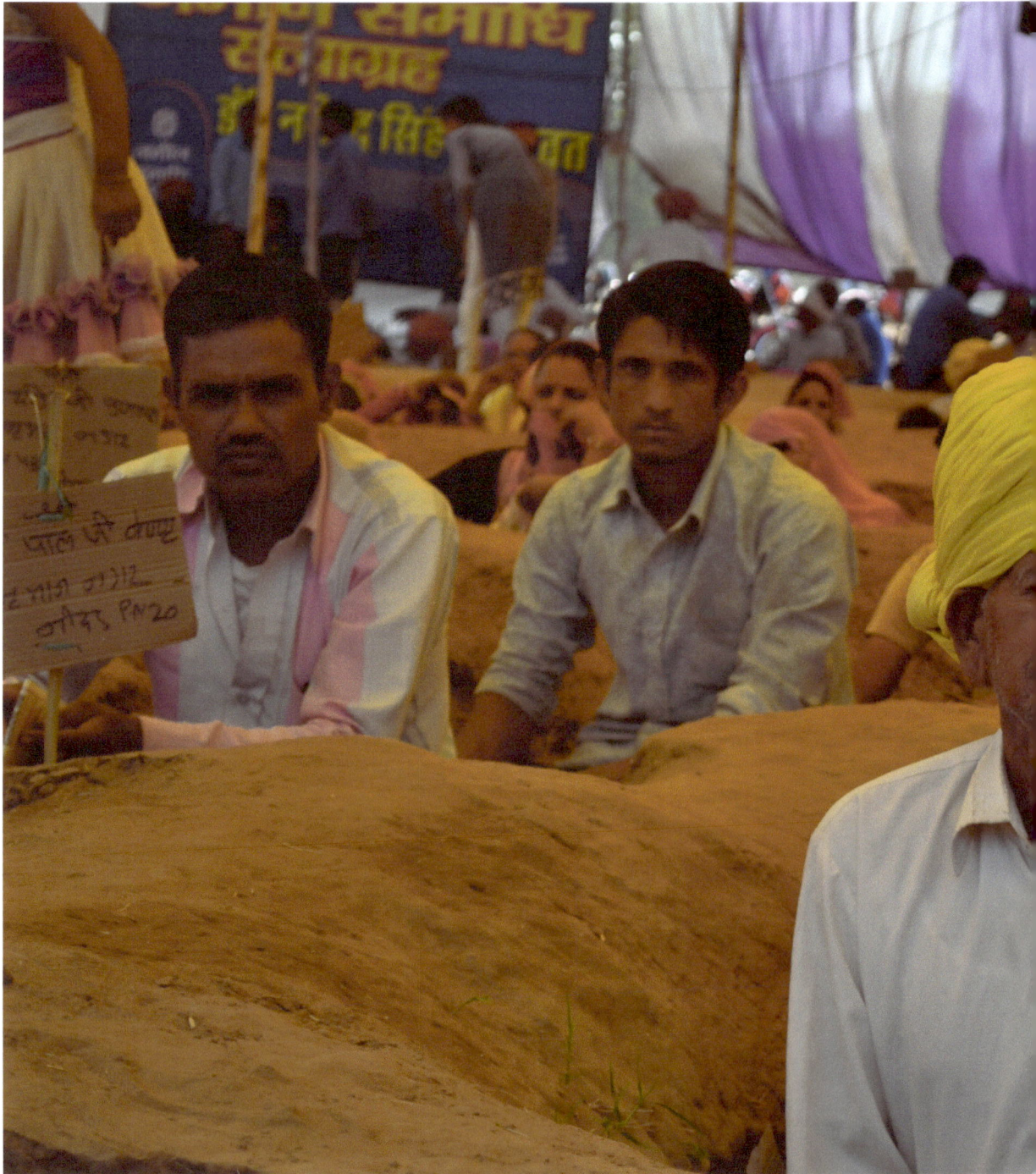

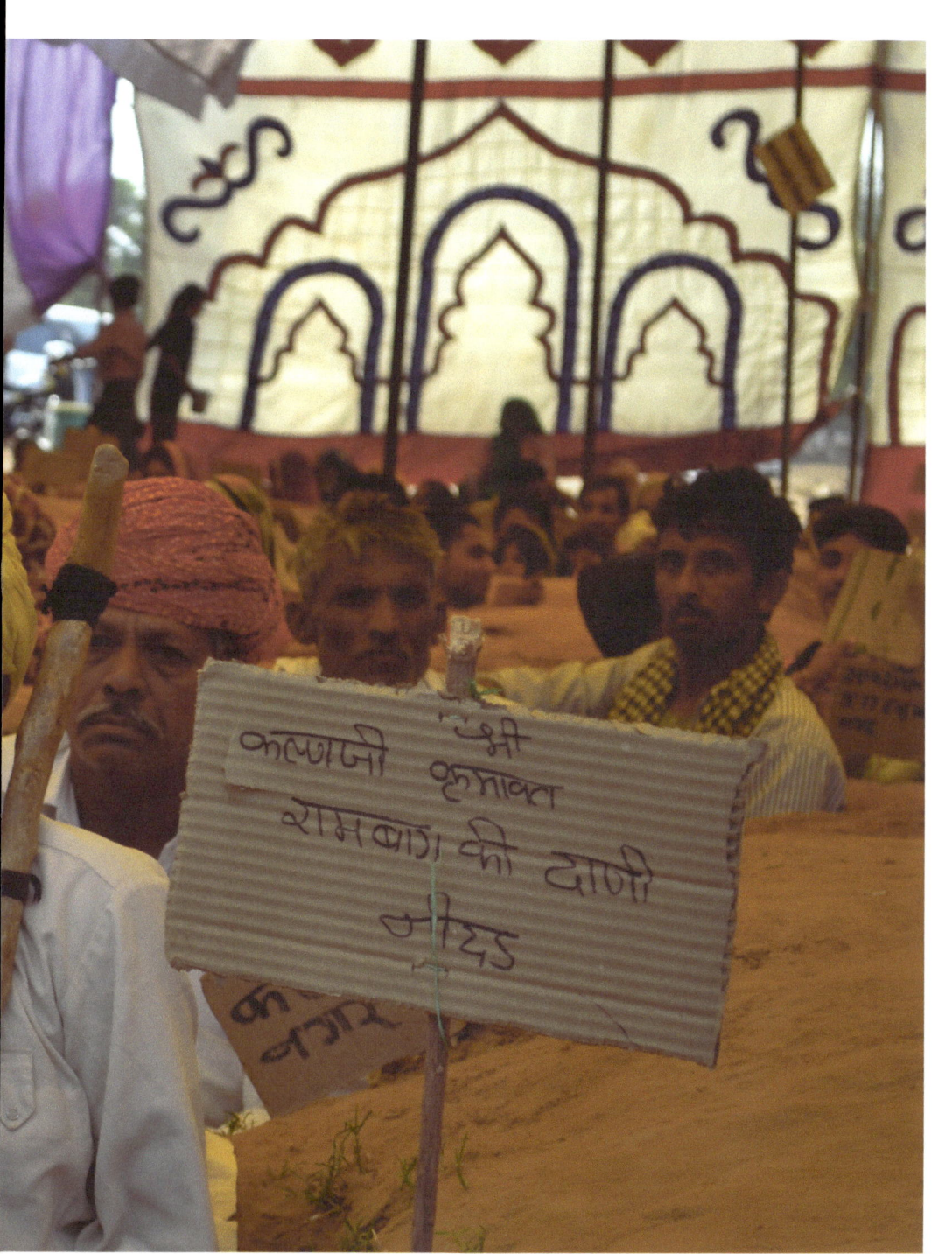

Protest of land Acquisitions in nidad

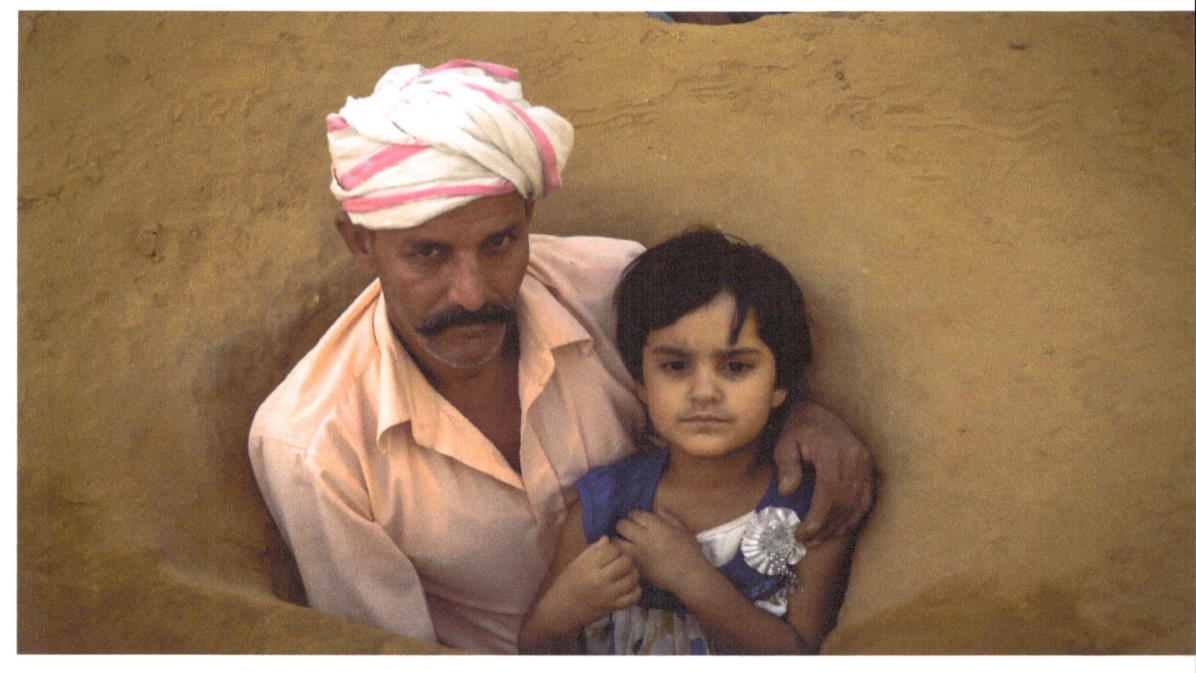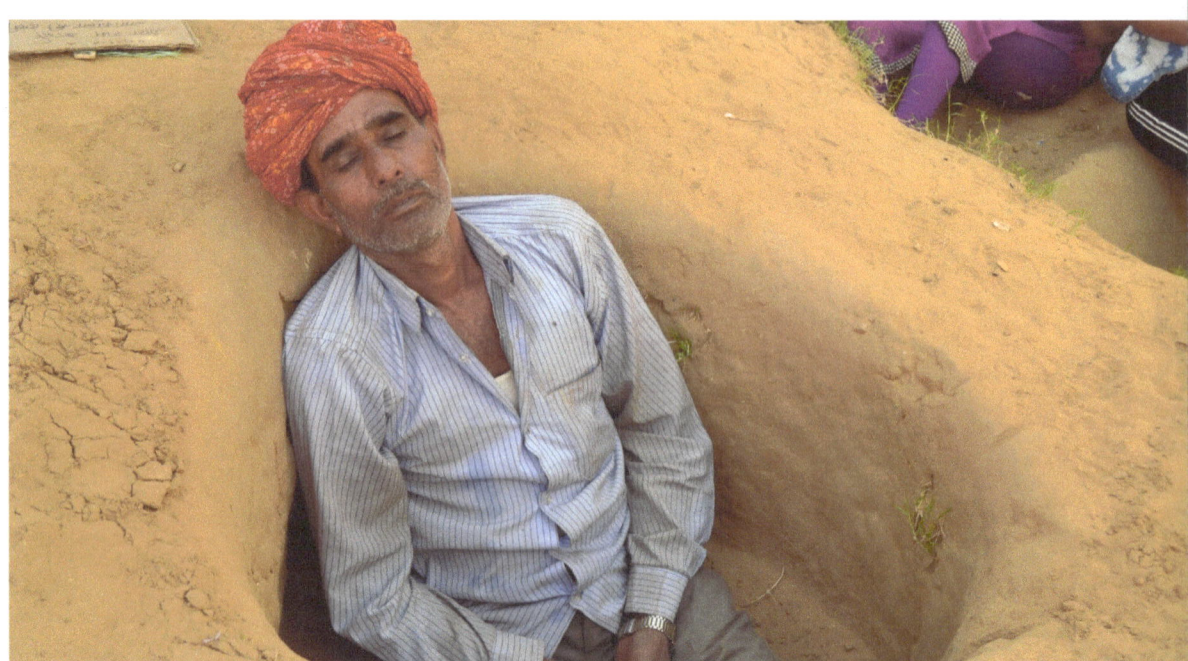

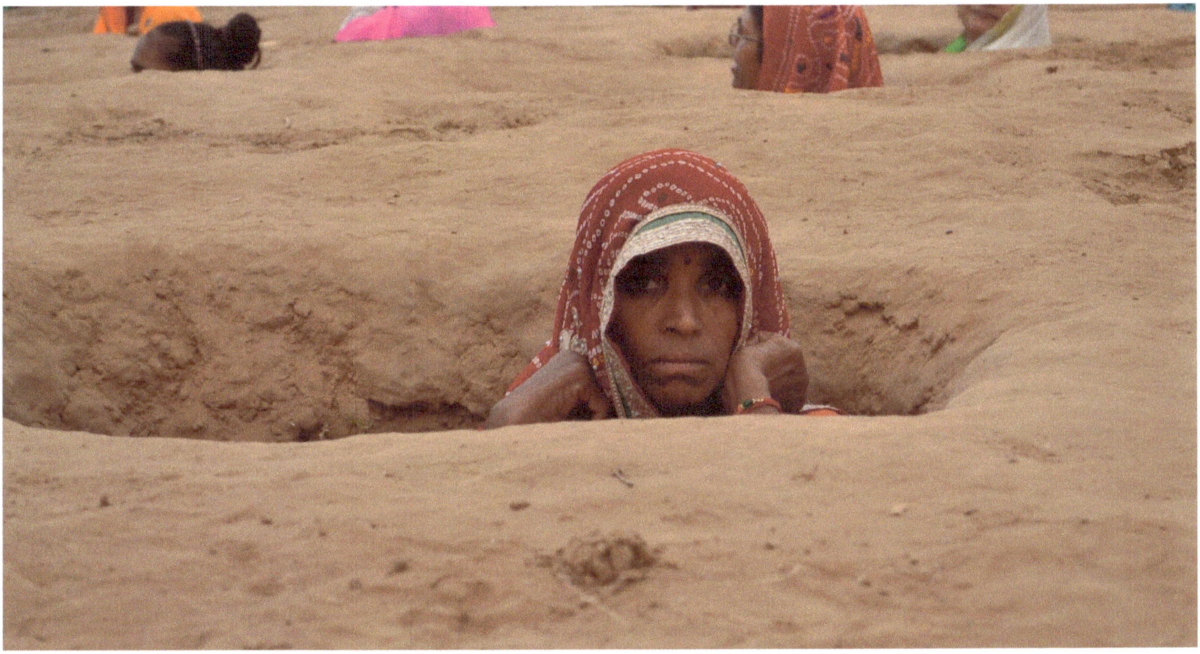

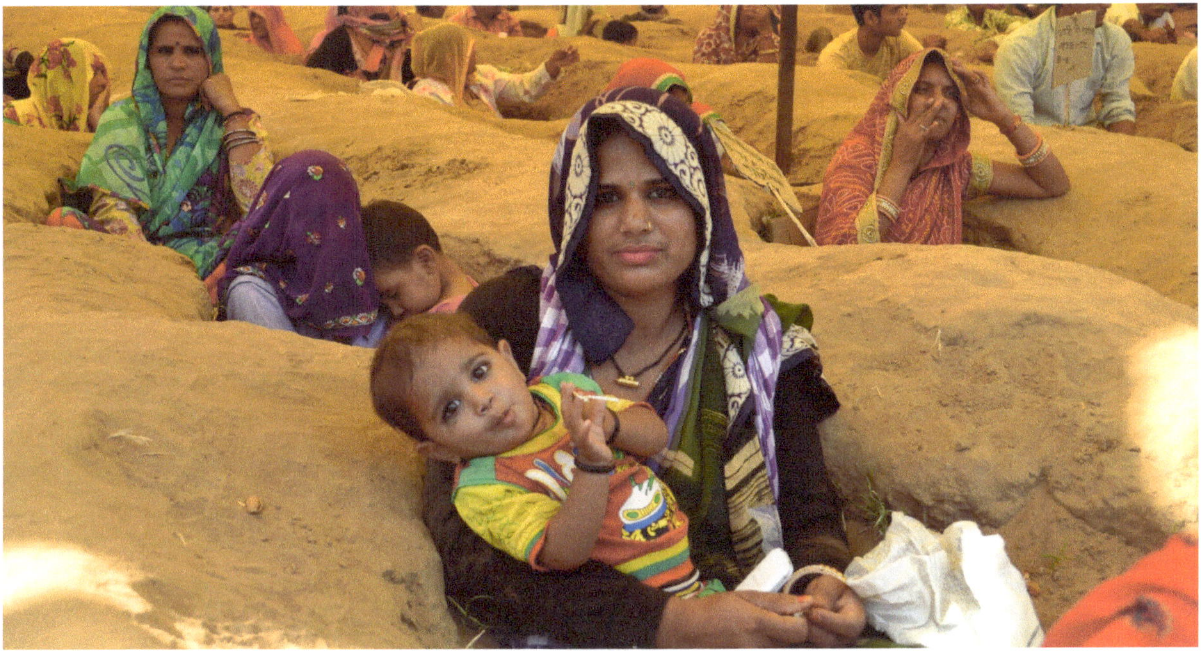

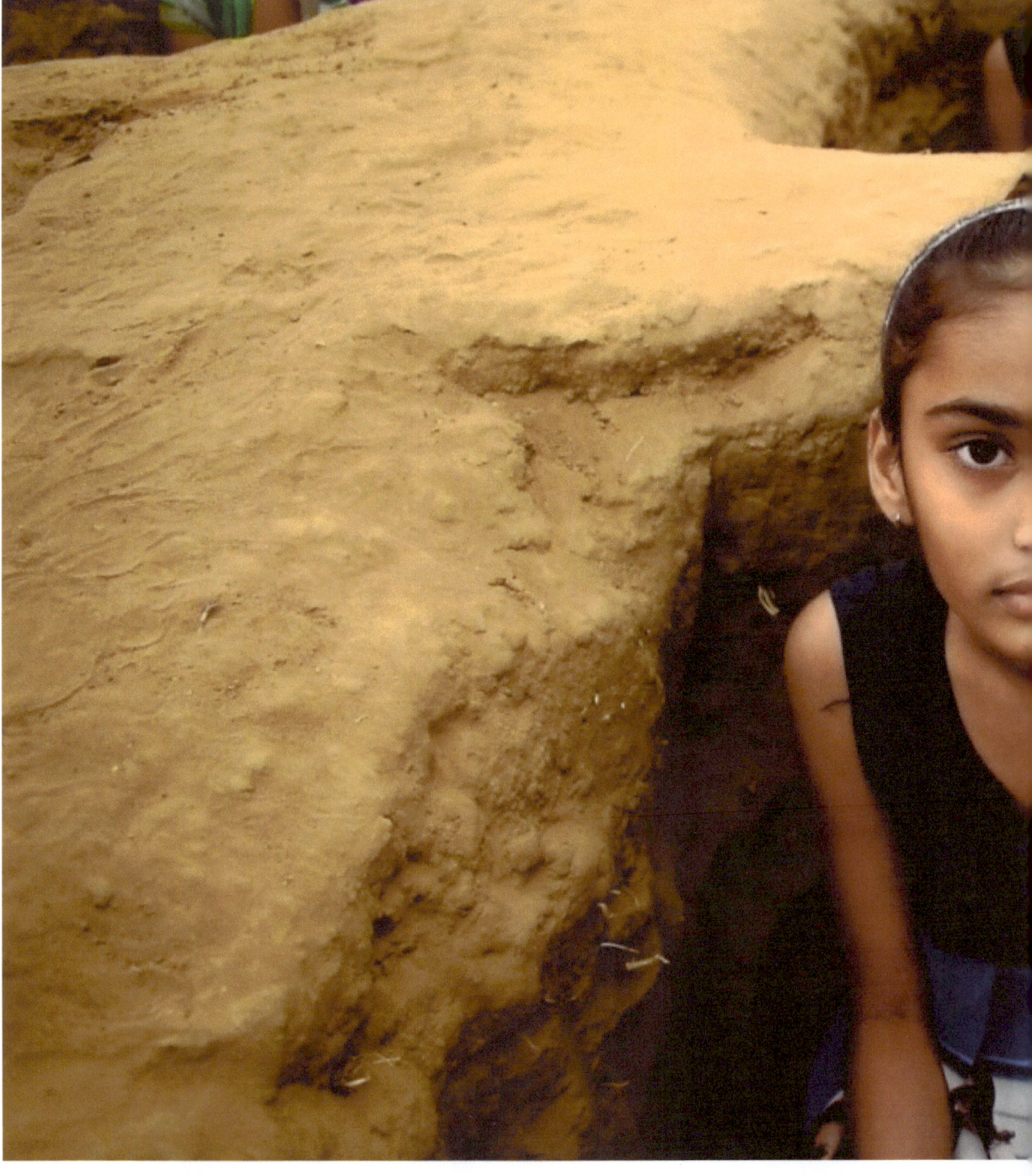

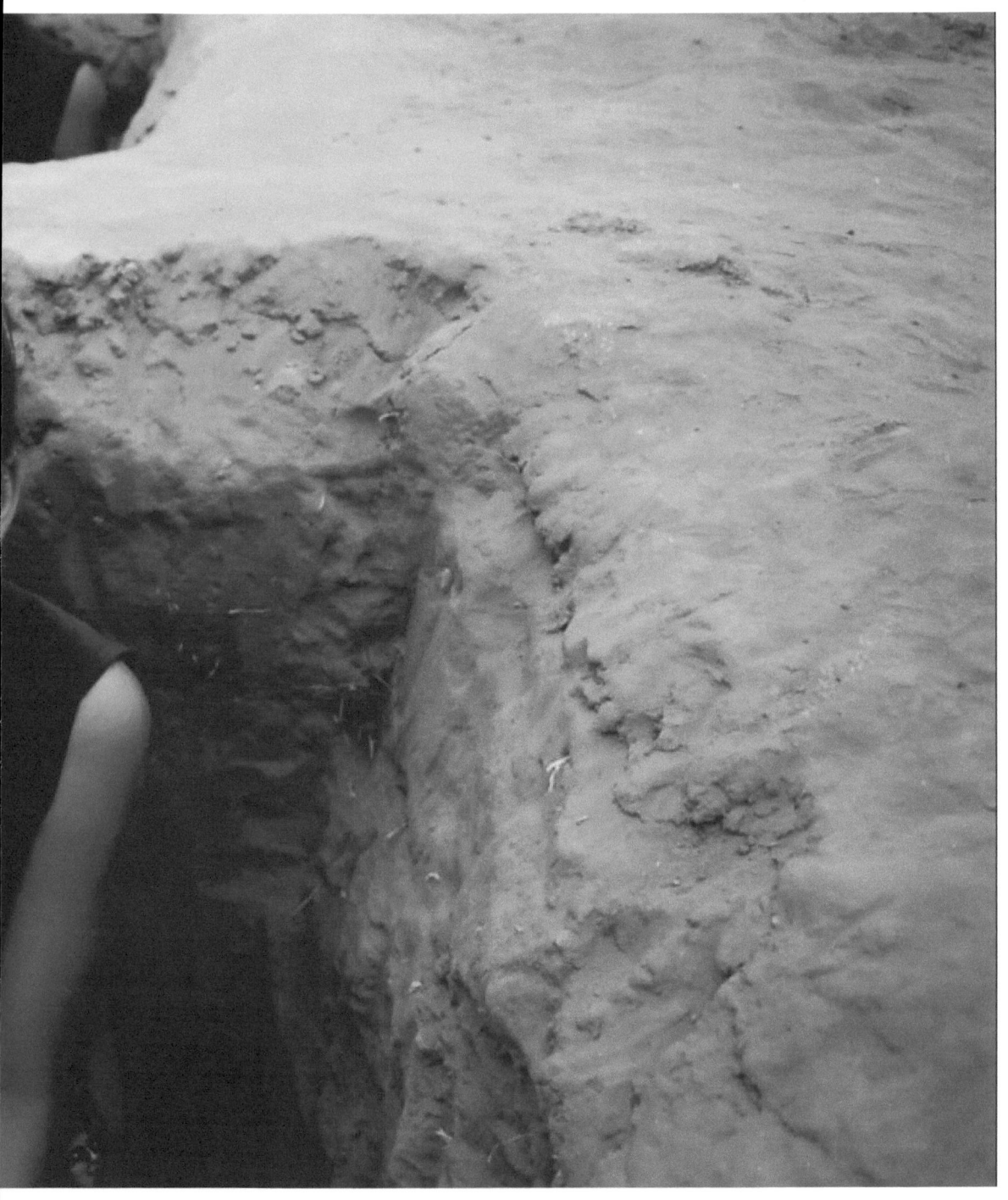

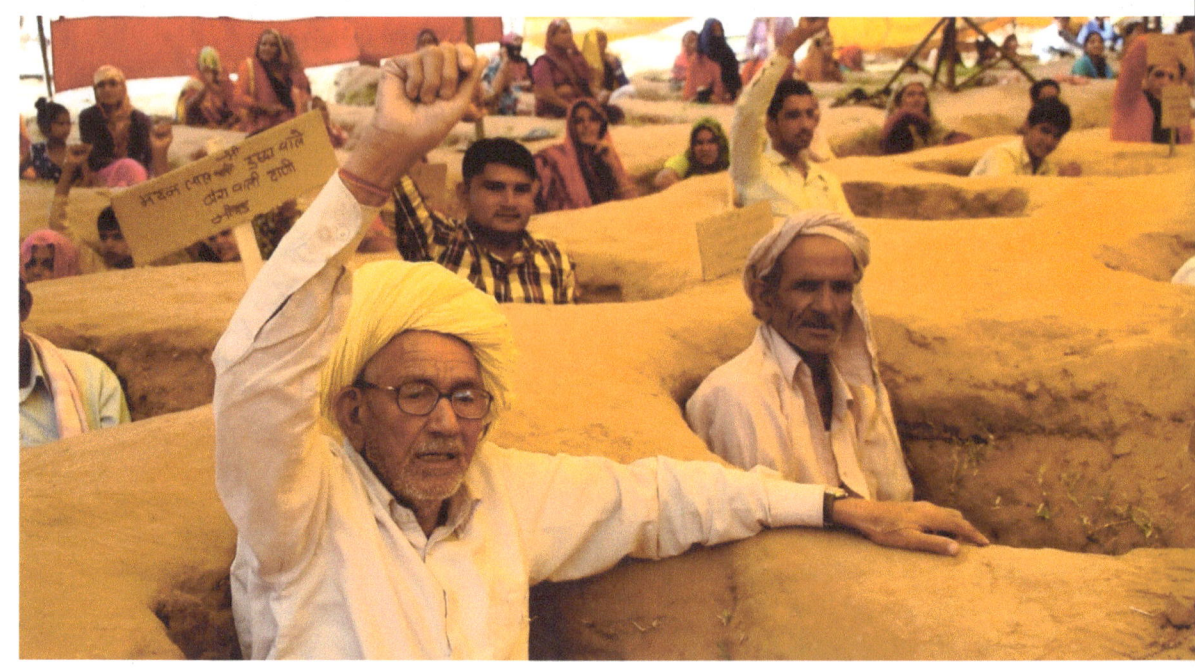
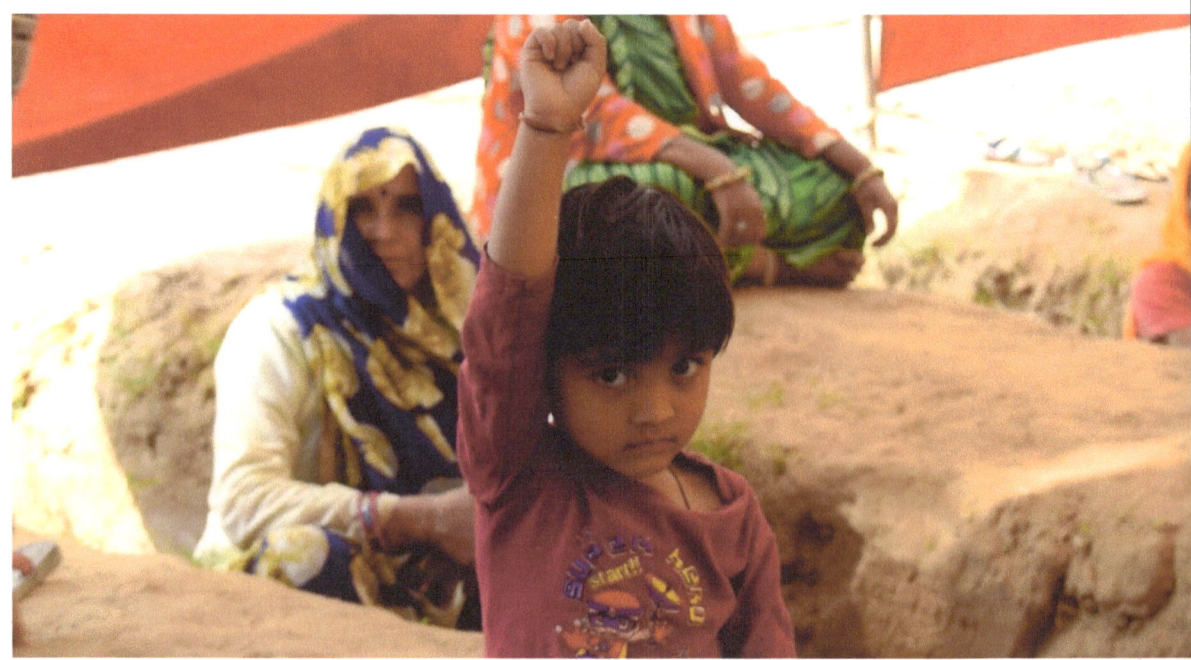

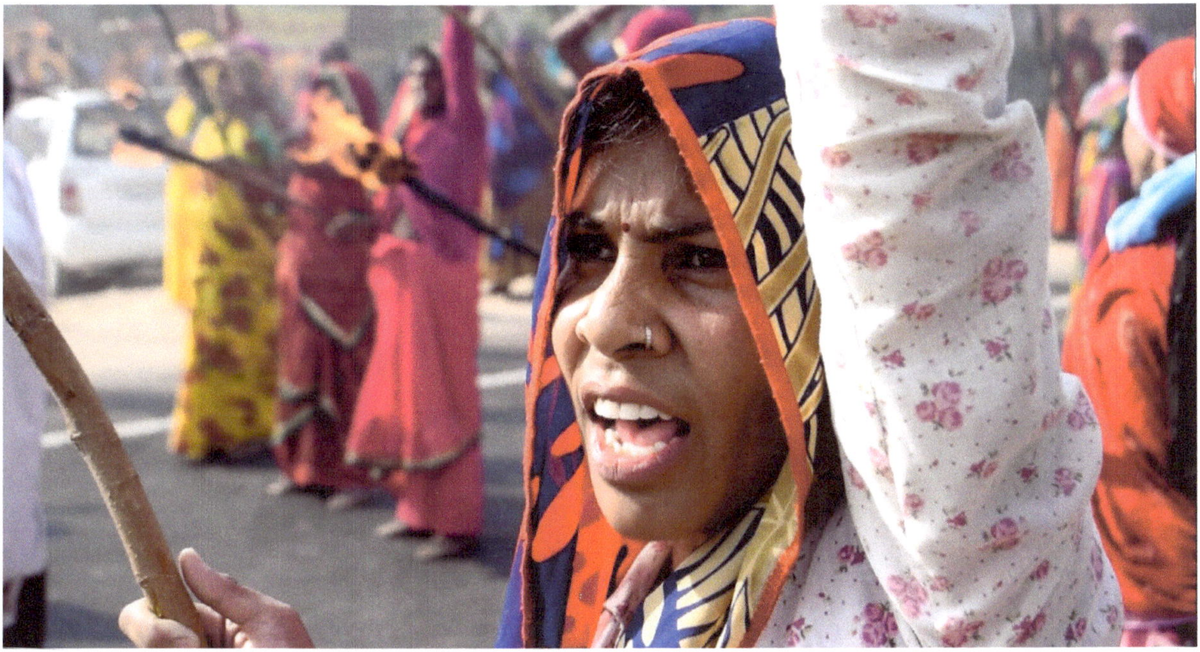

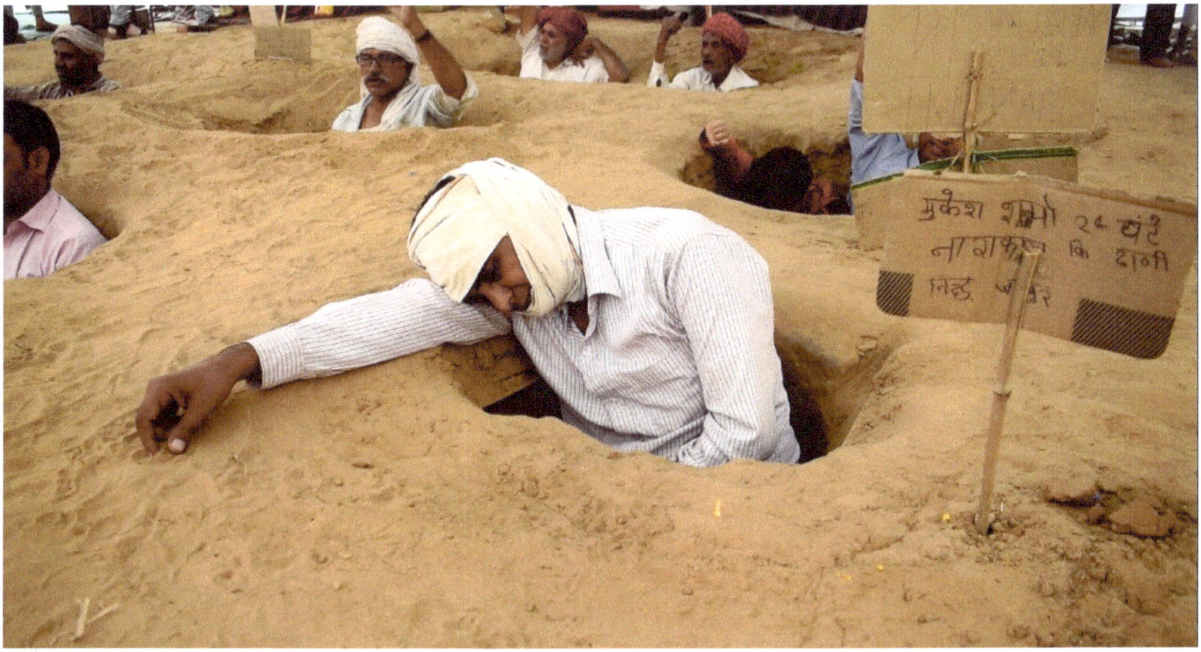

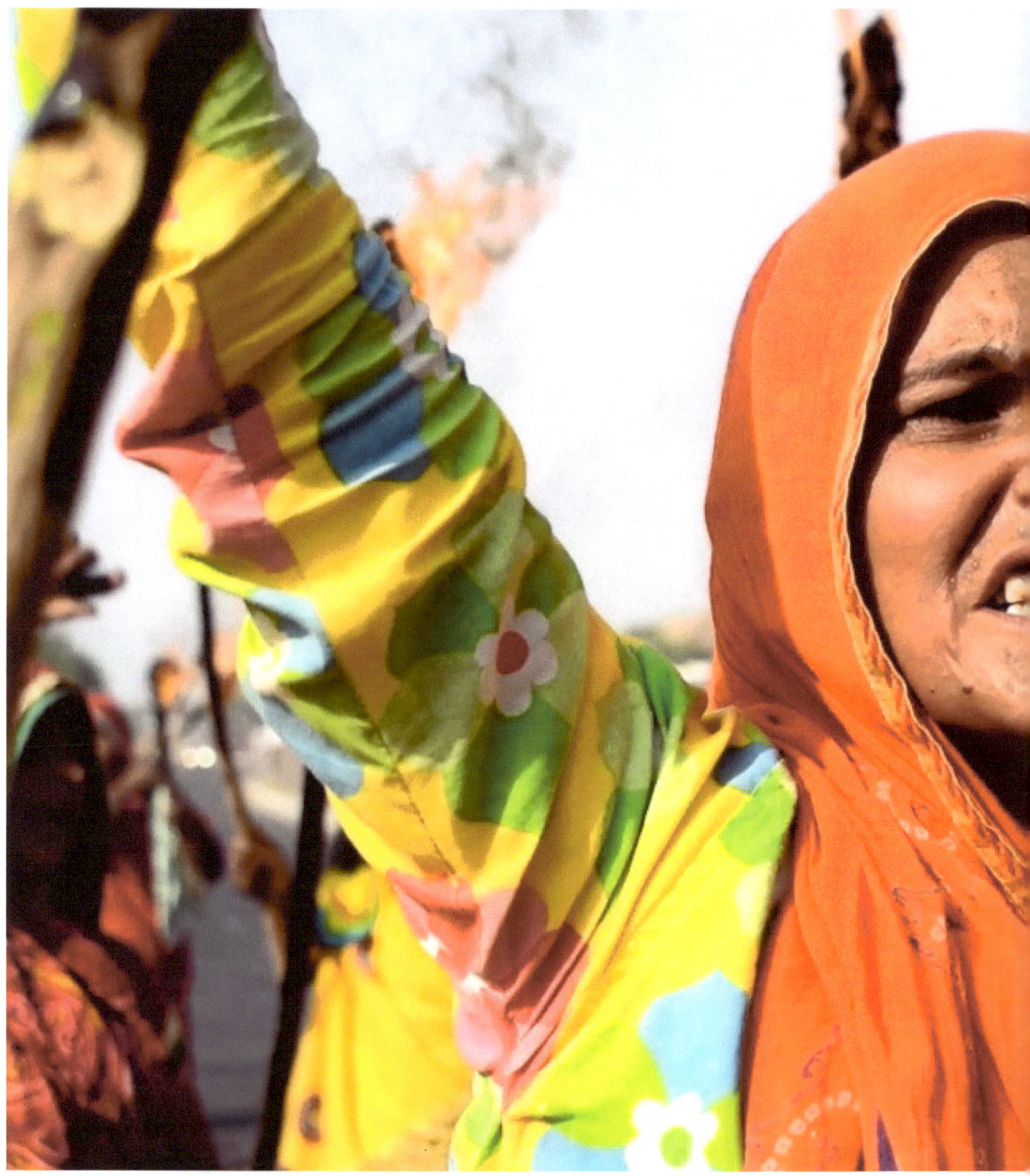

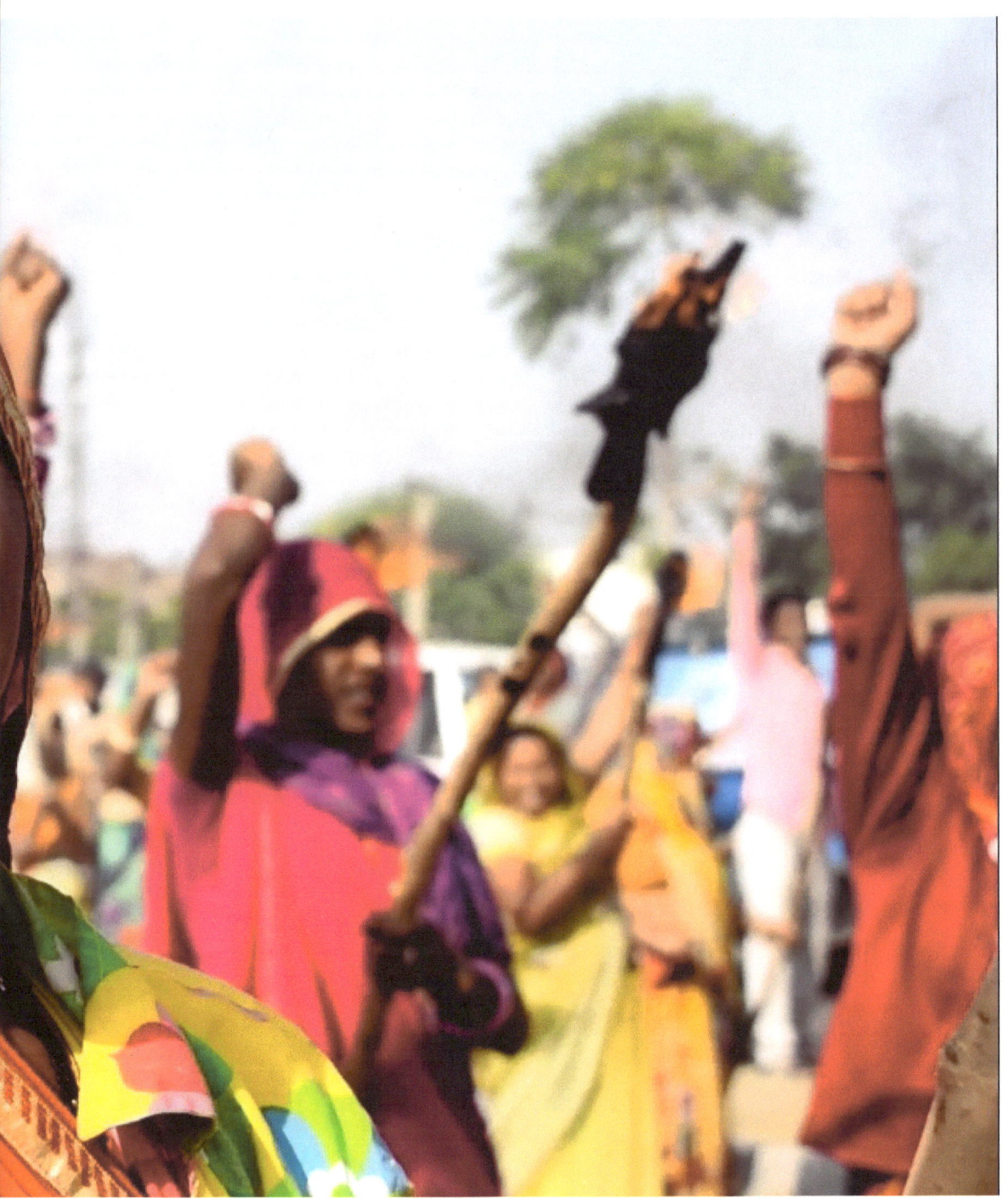

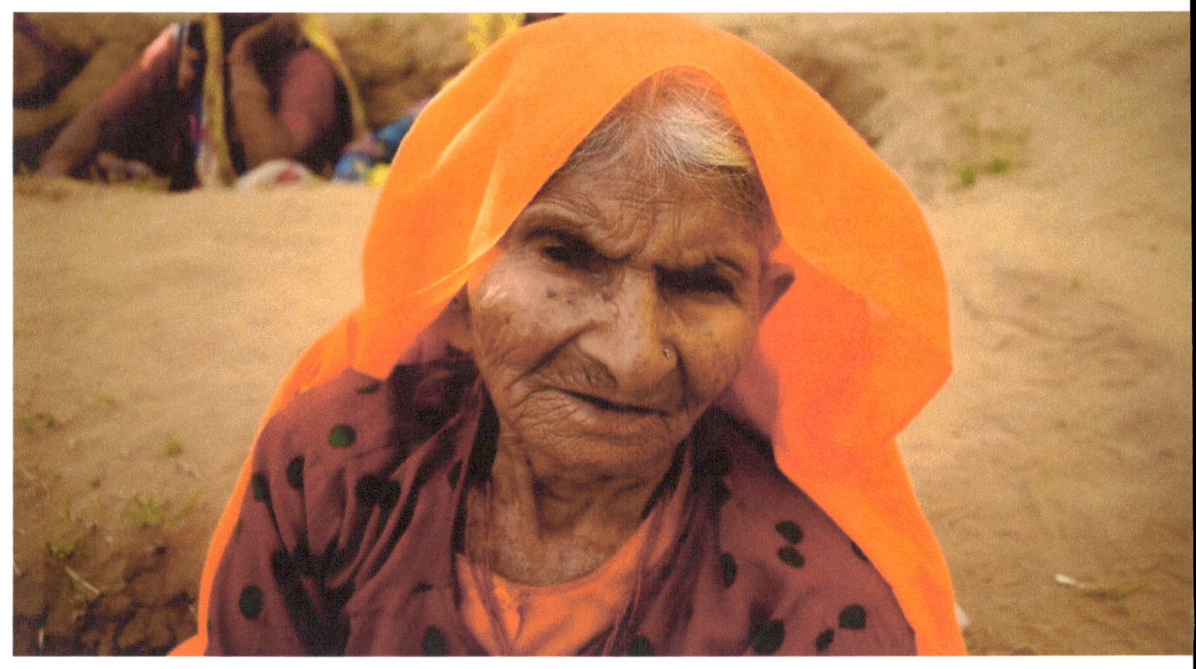

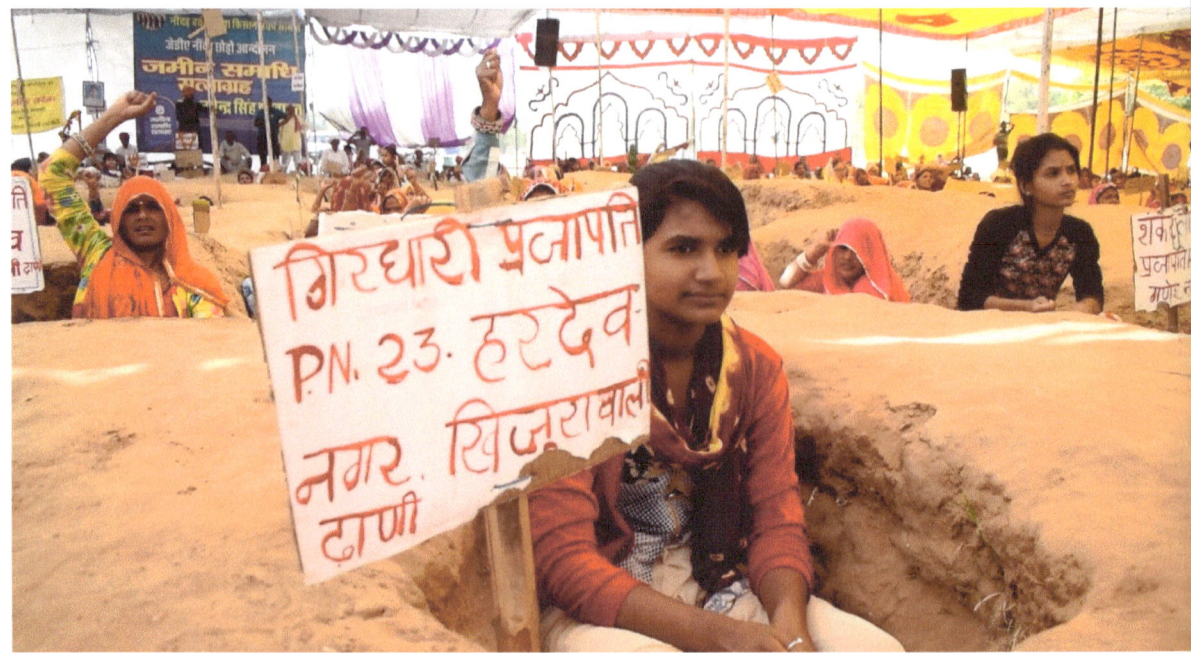

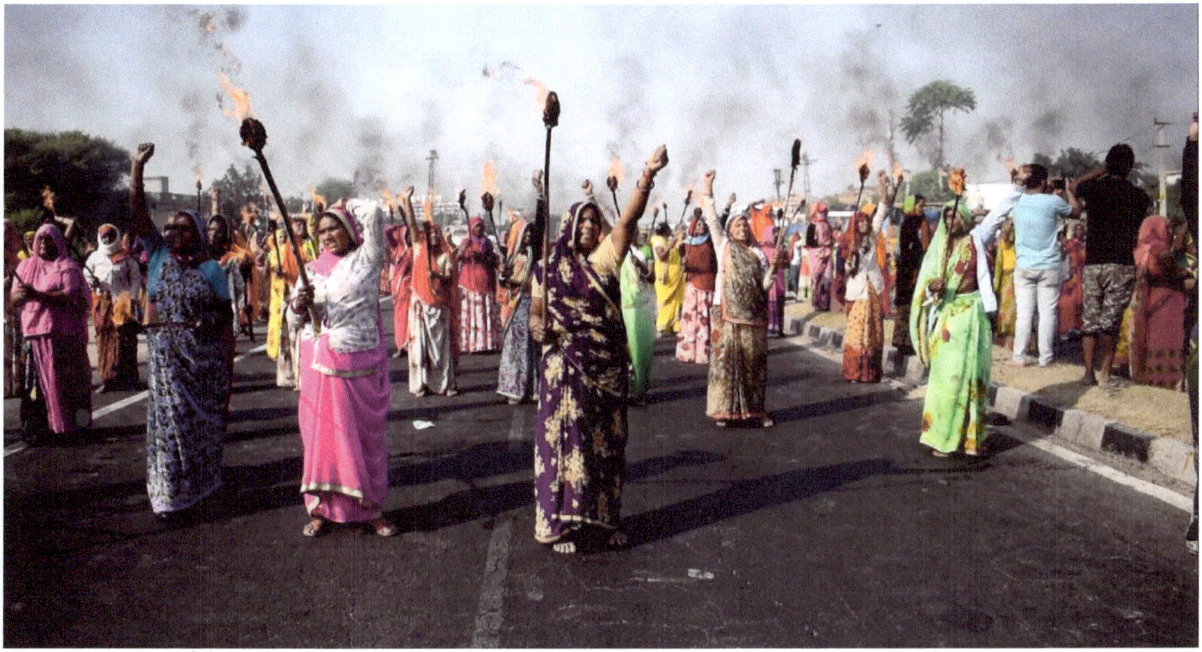

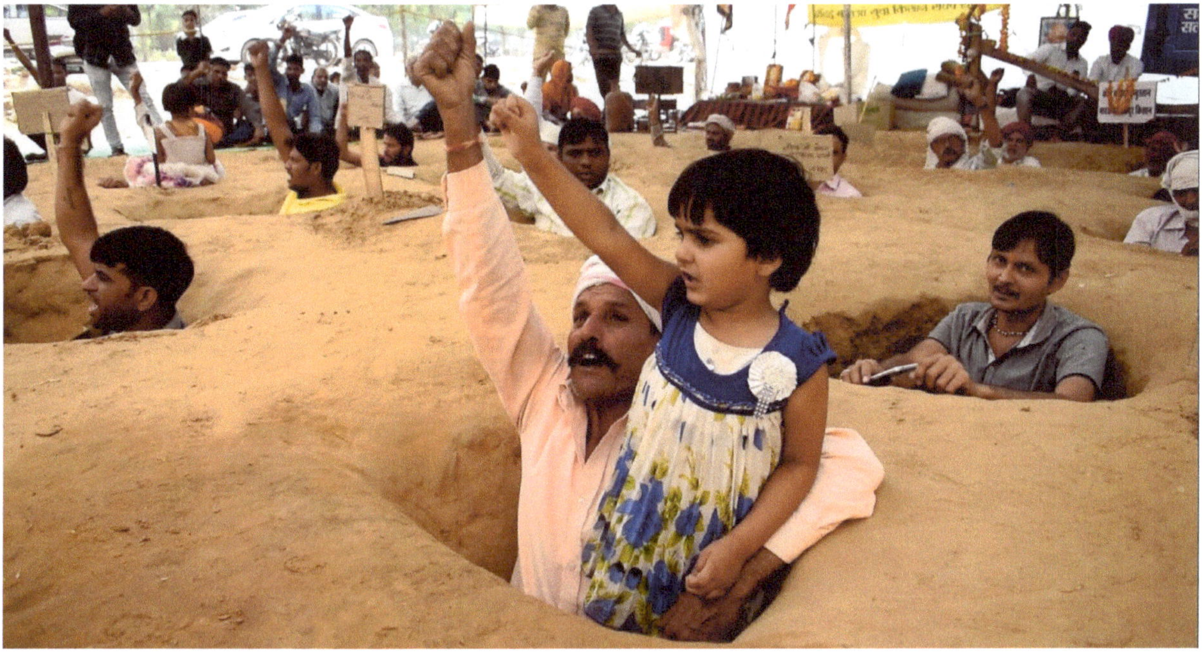

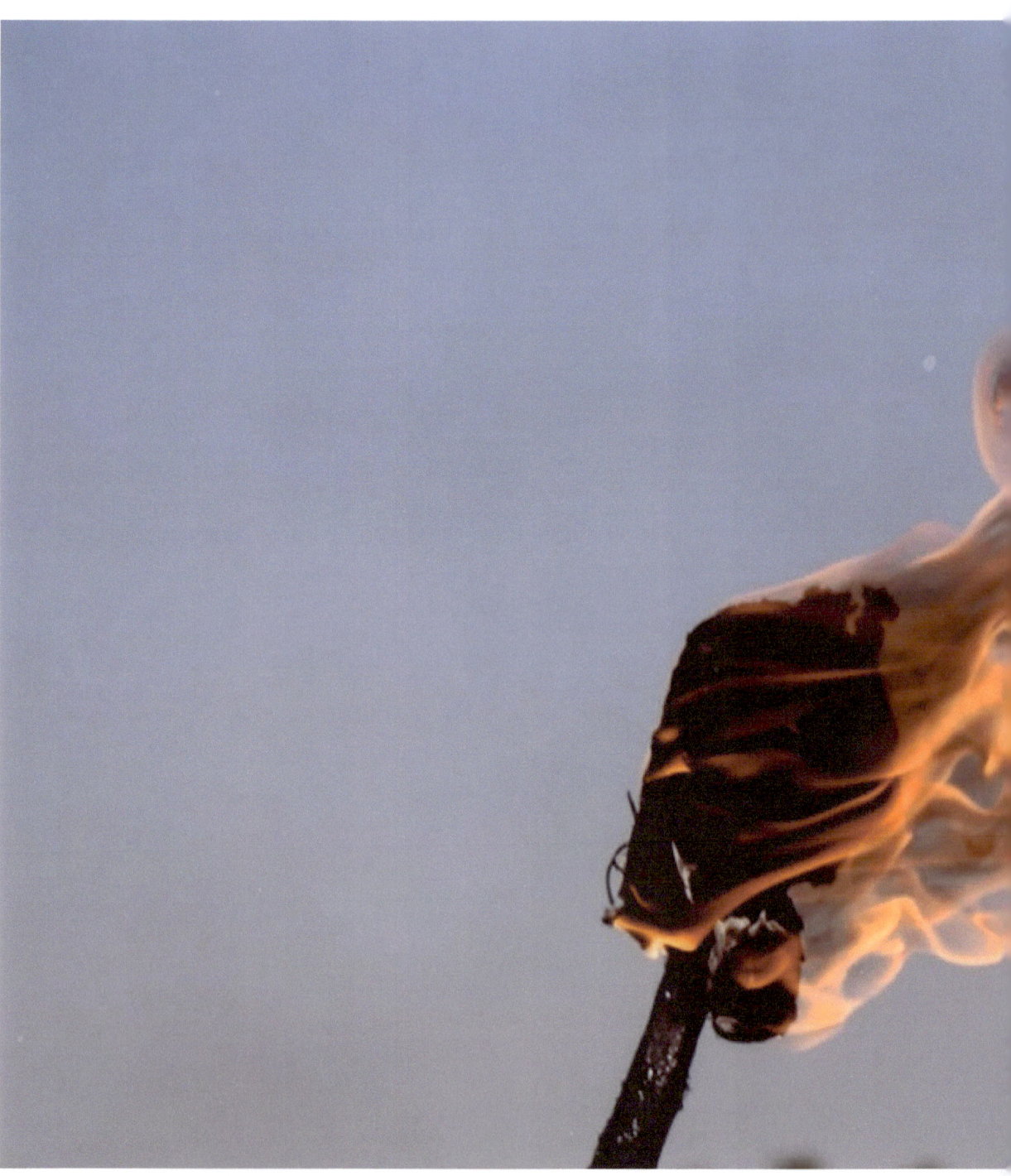

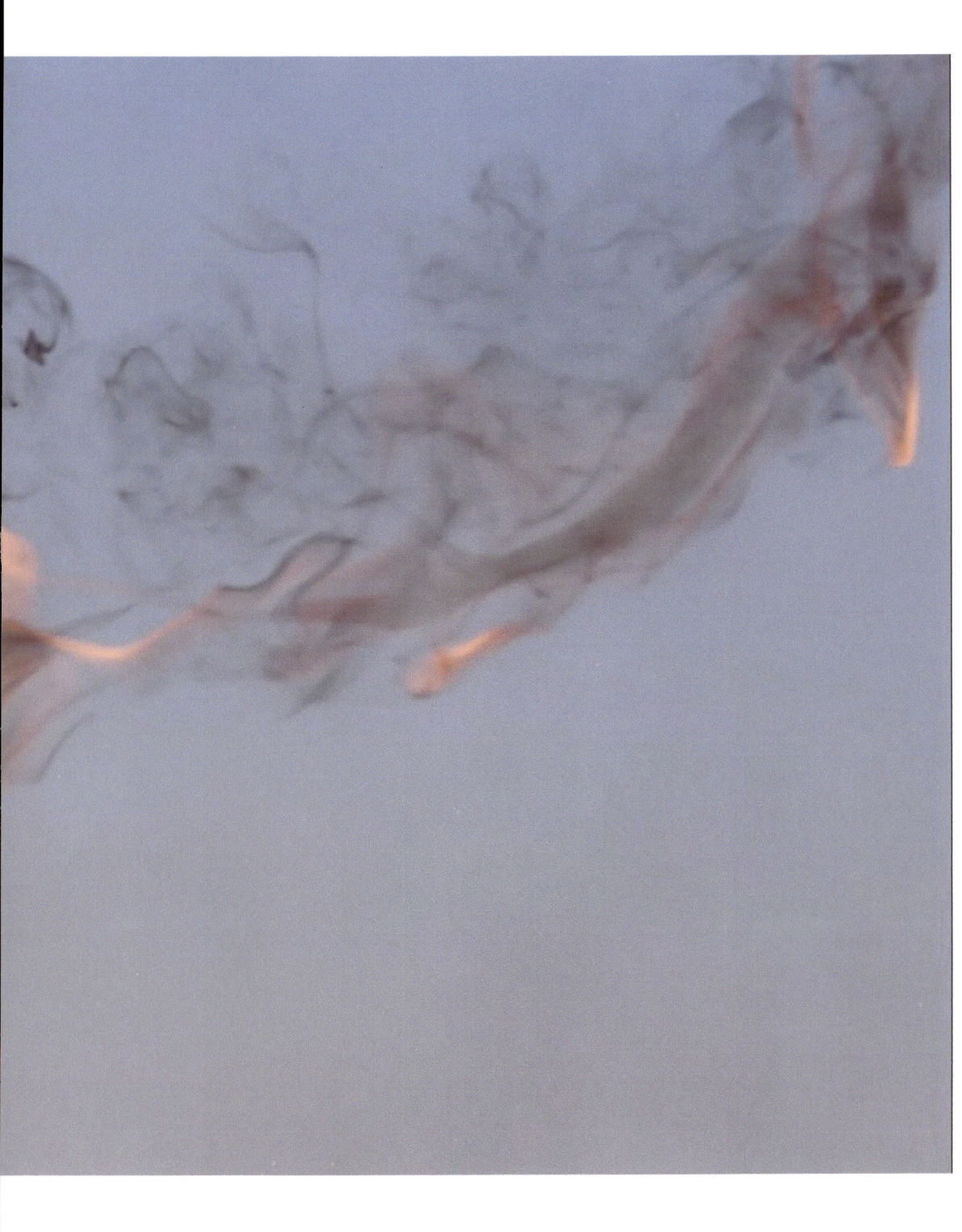

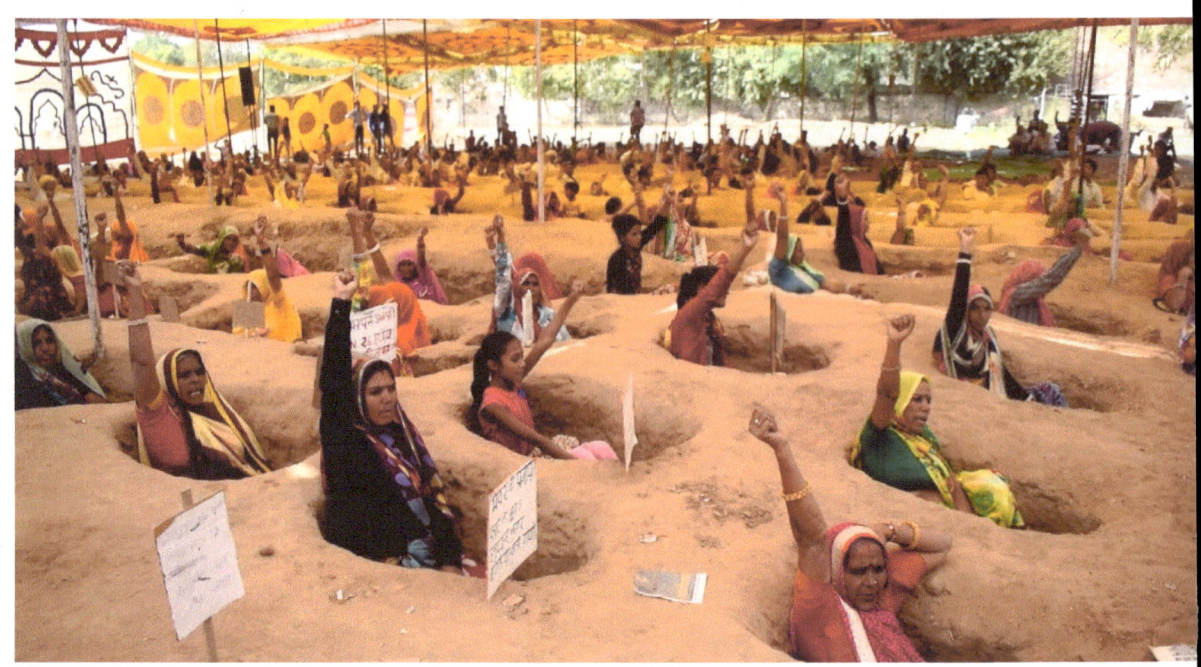

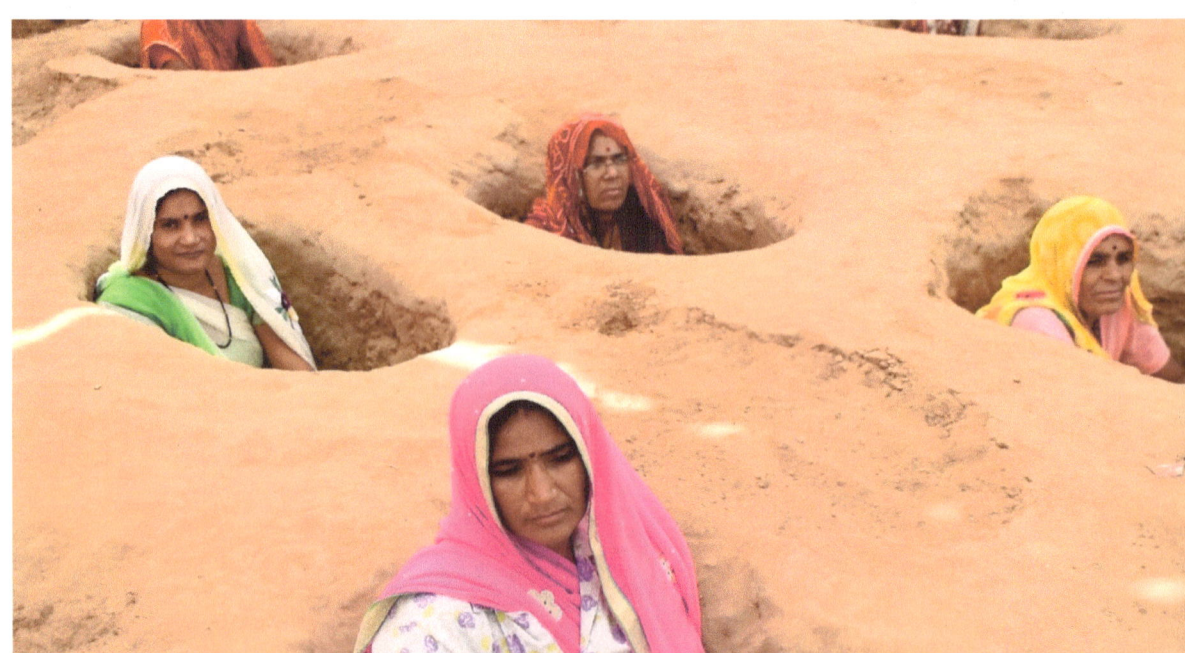

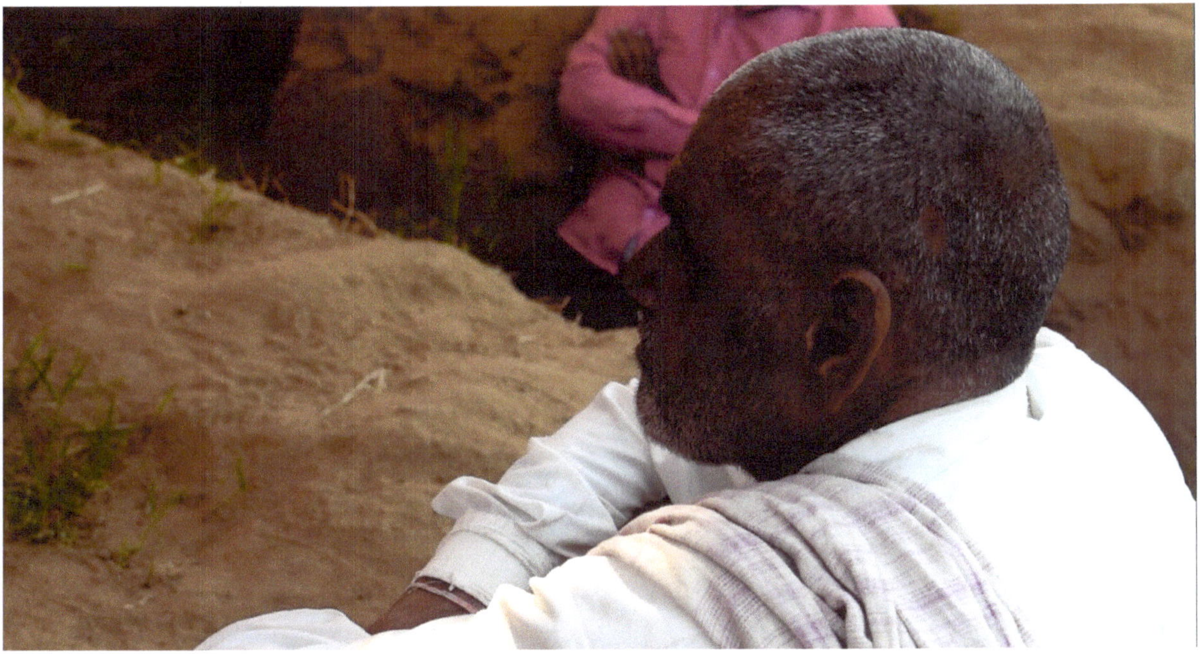

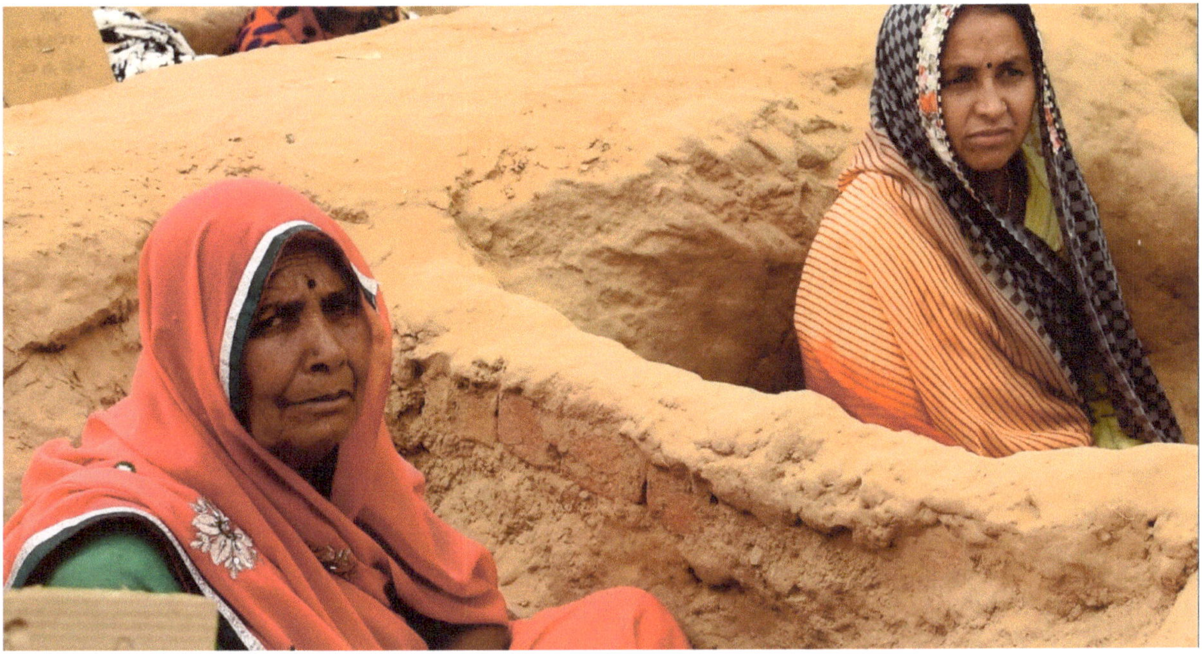

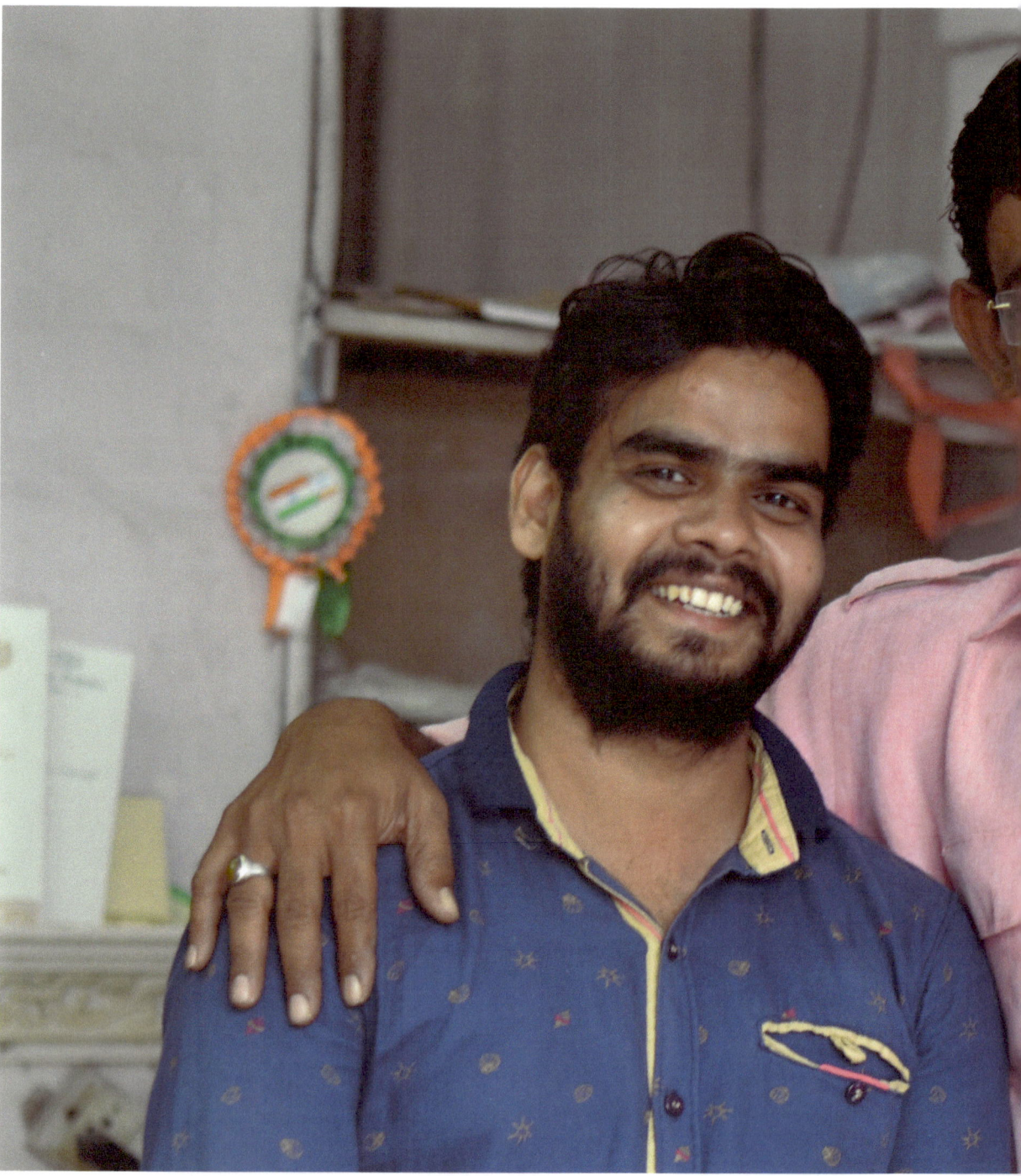

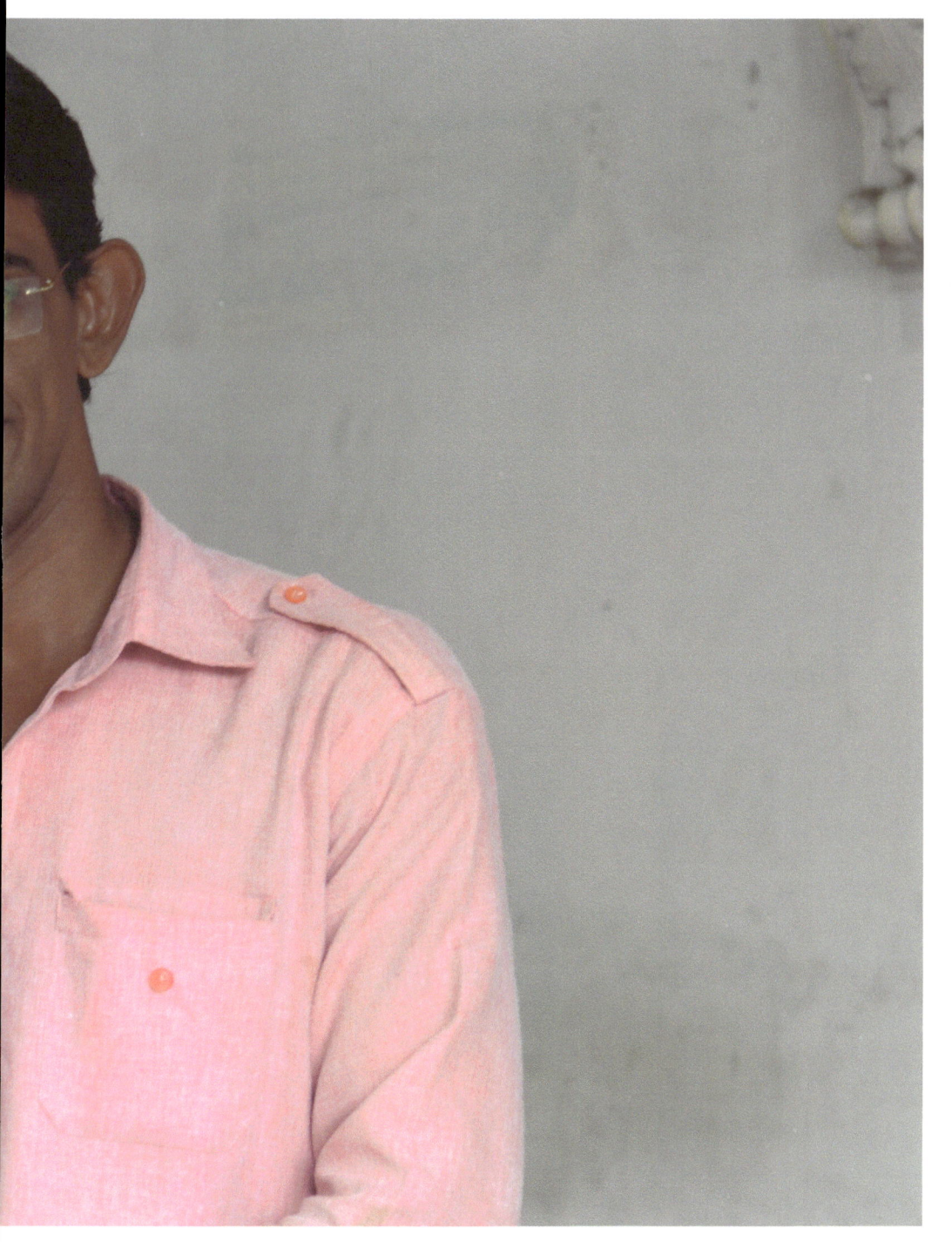

Memories of Hyderabad

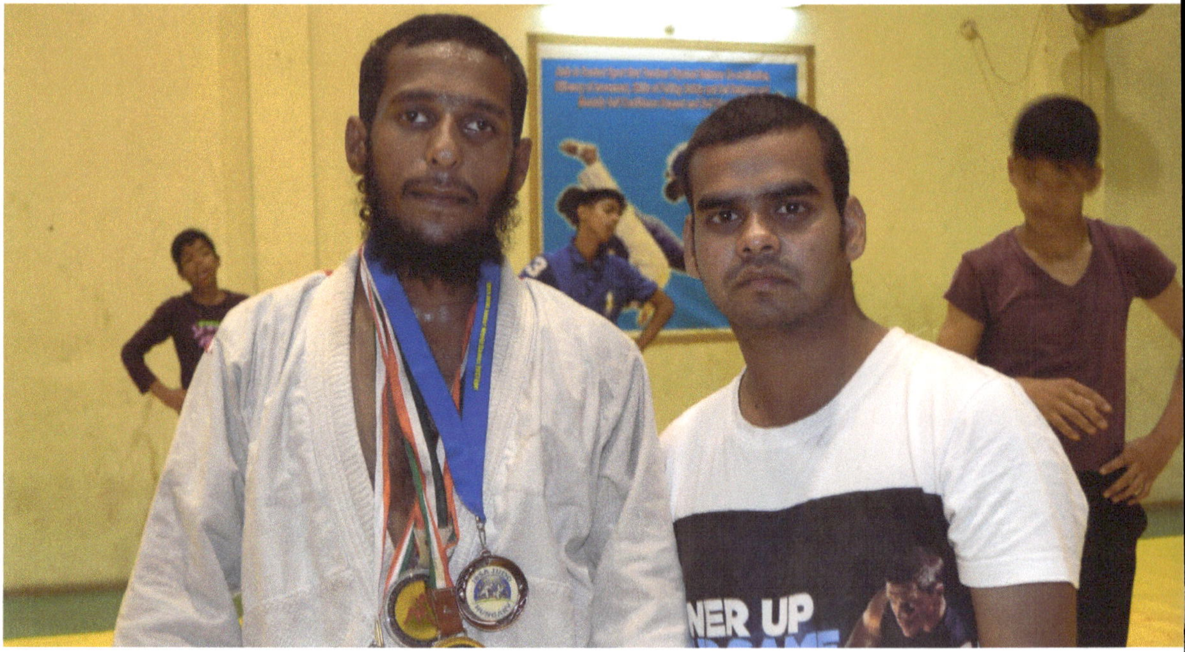

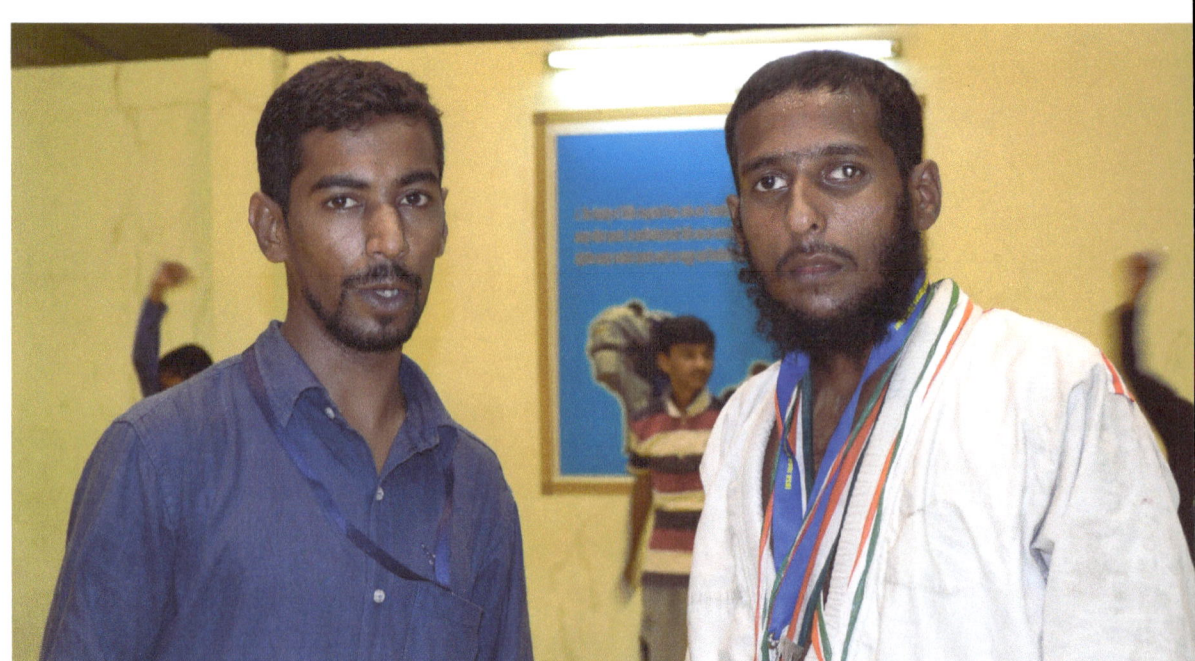

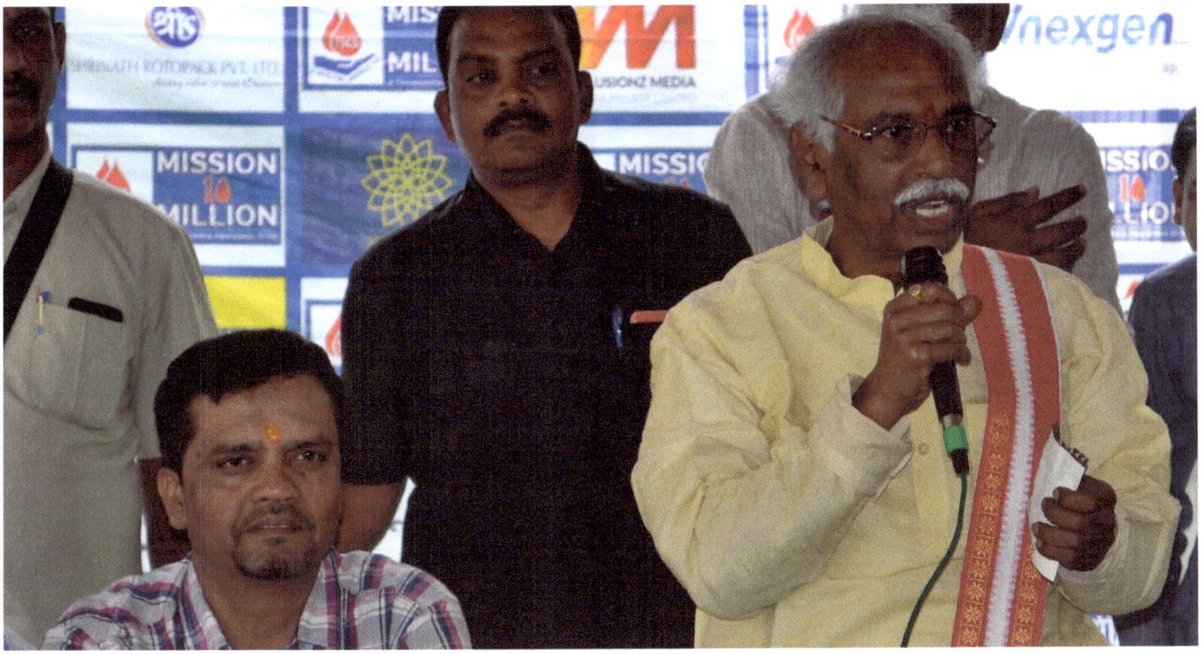

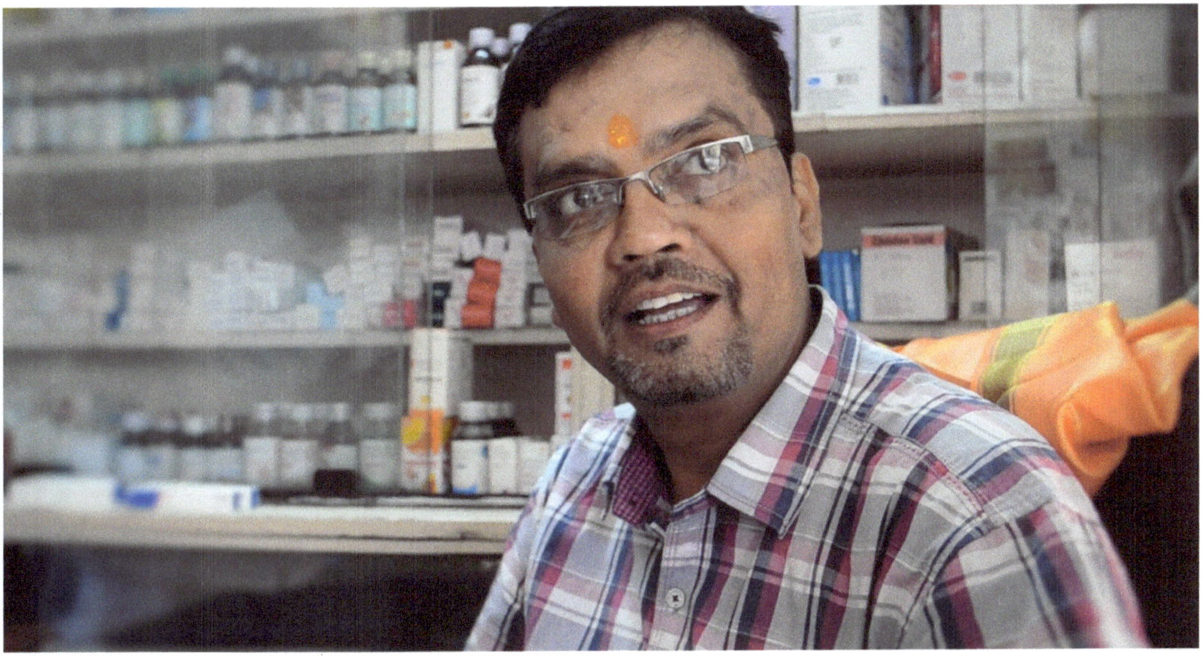

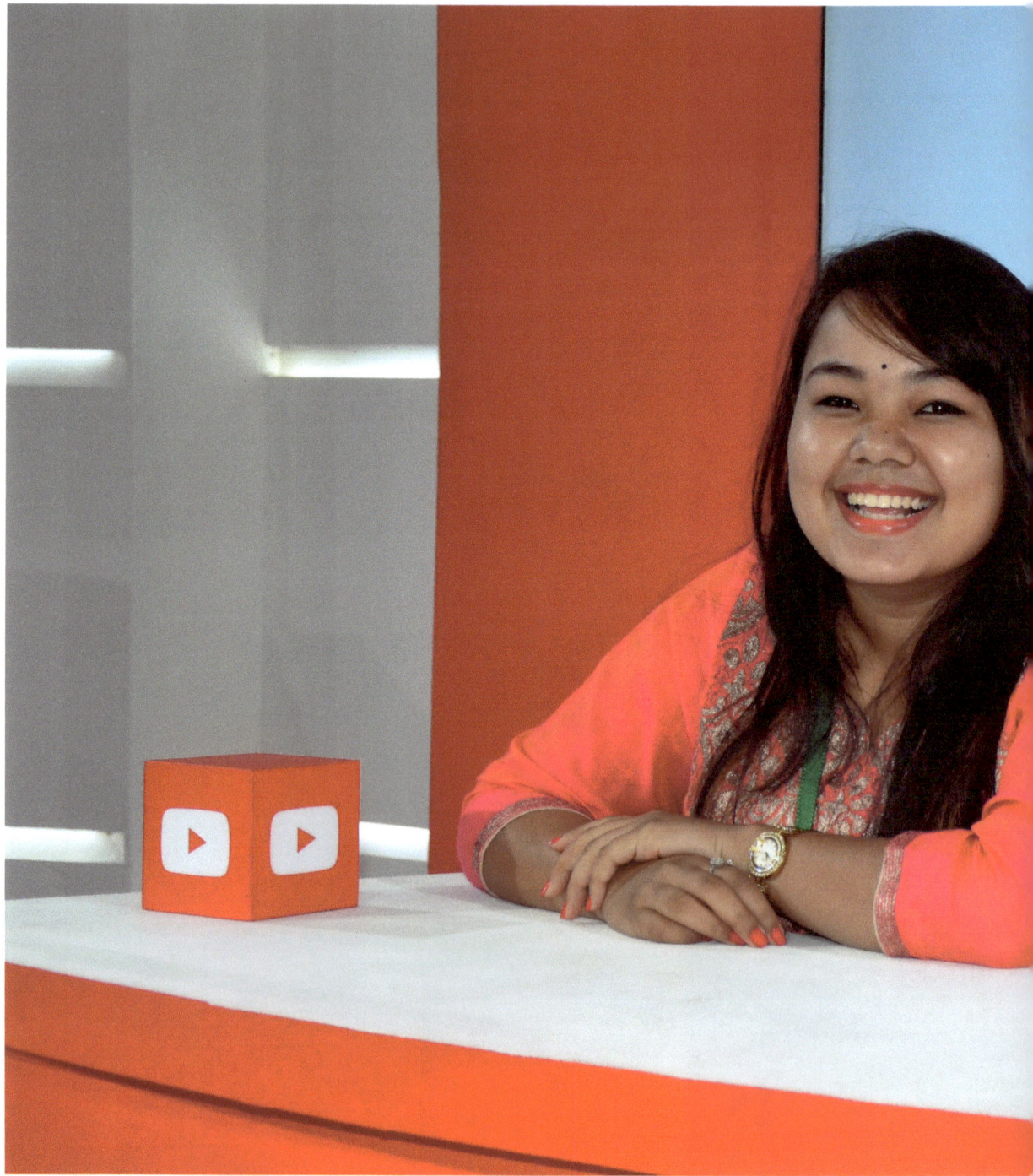

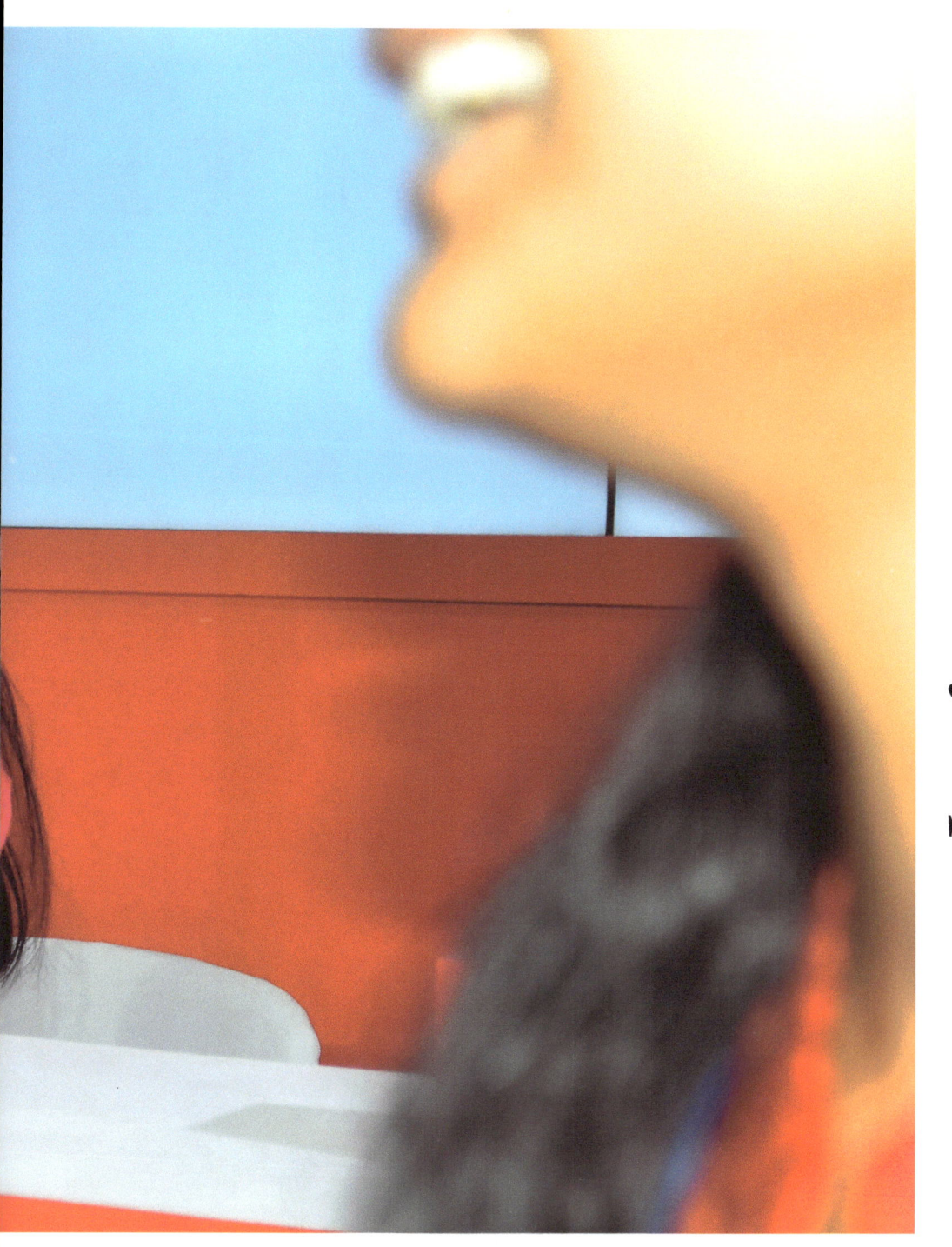

Memories of Jaipur

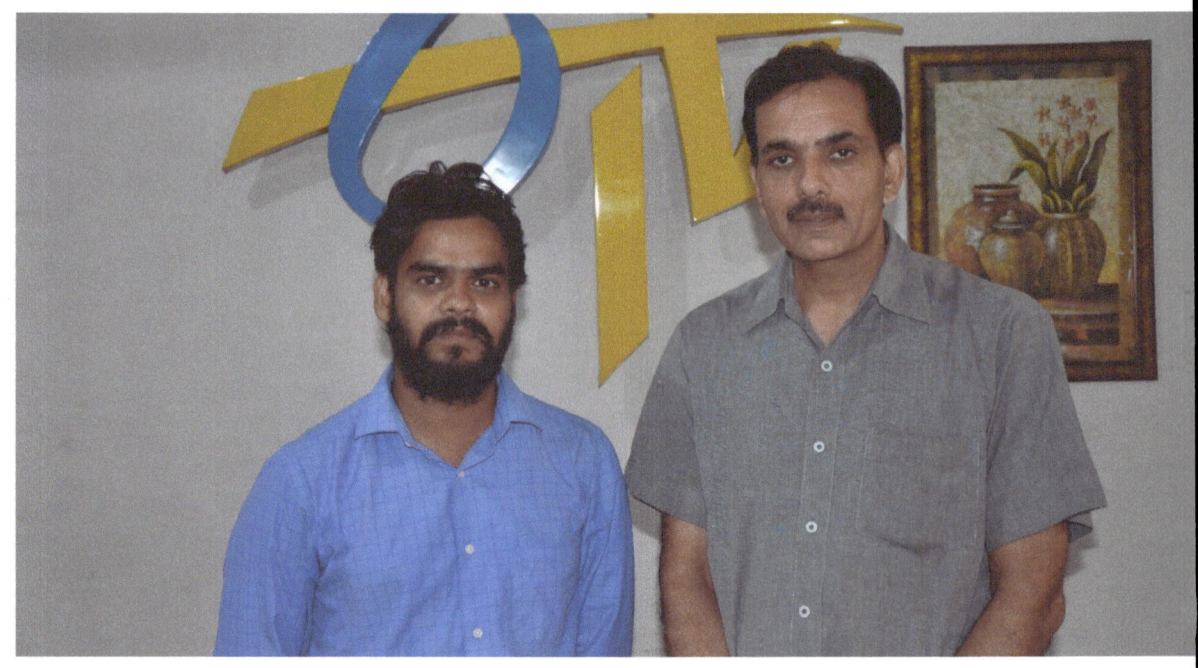
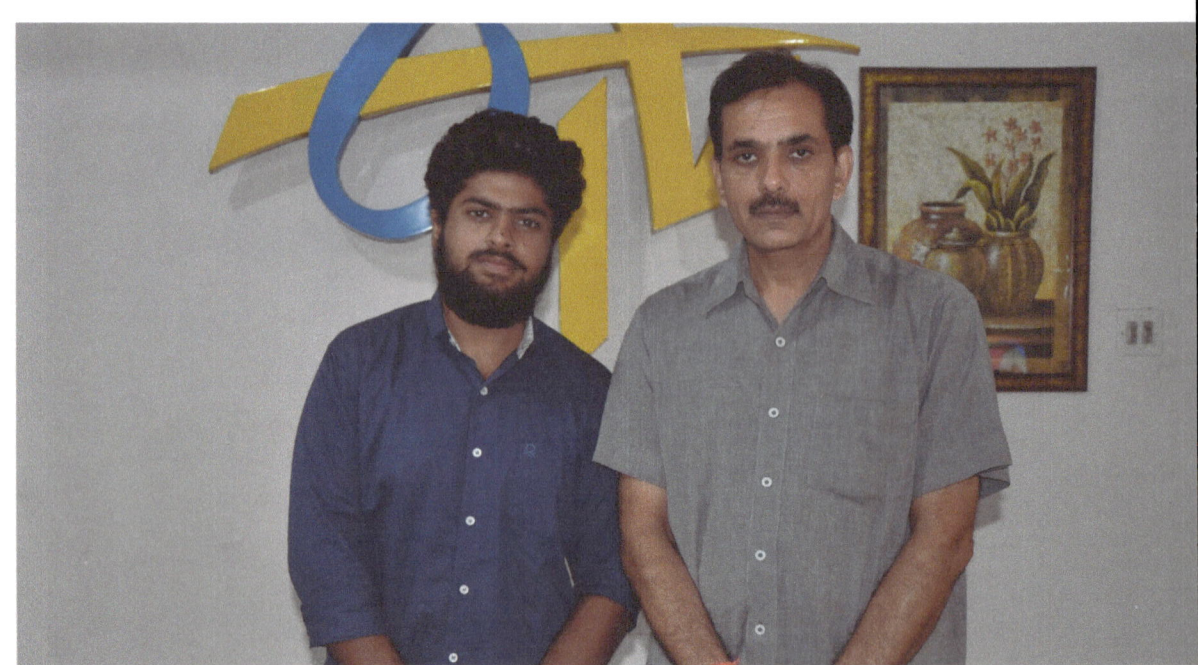

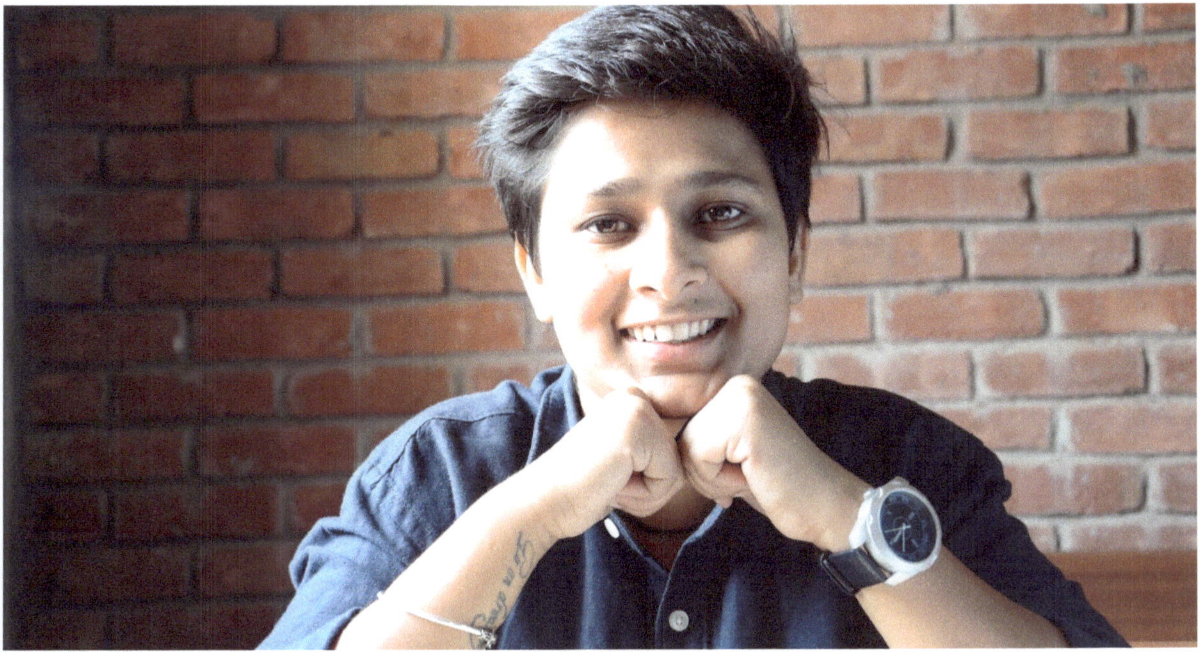

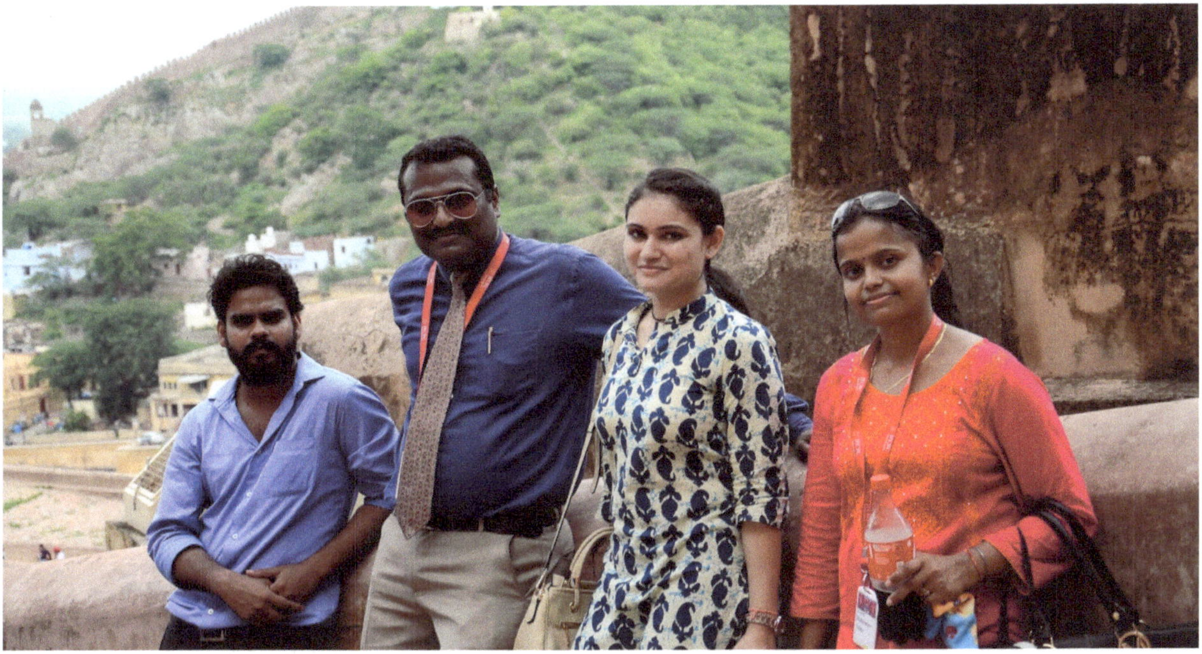

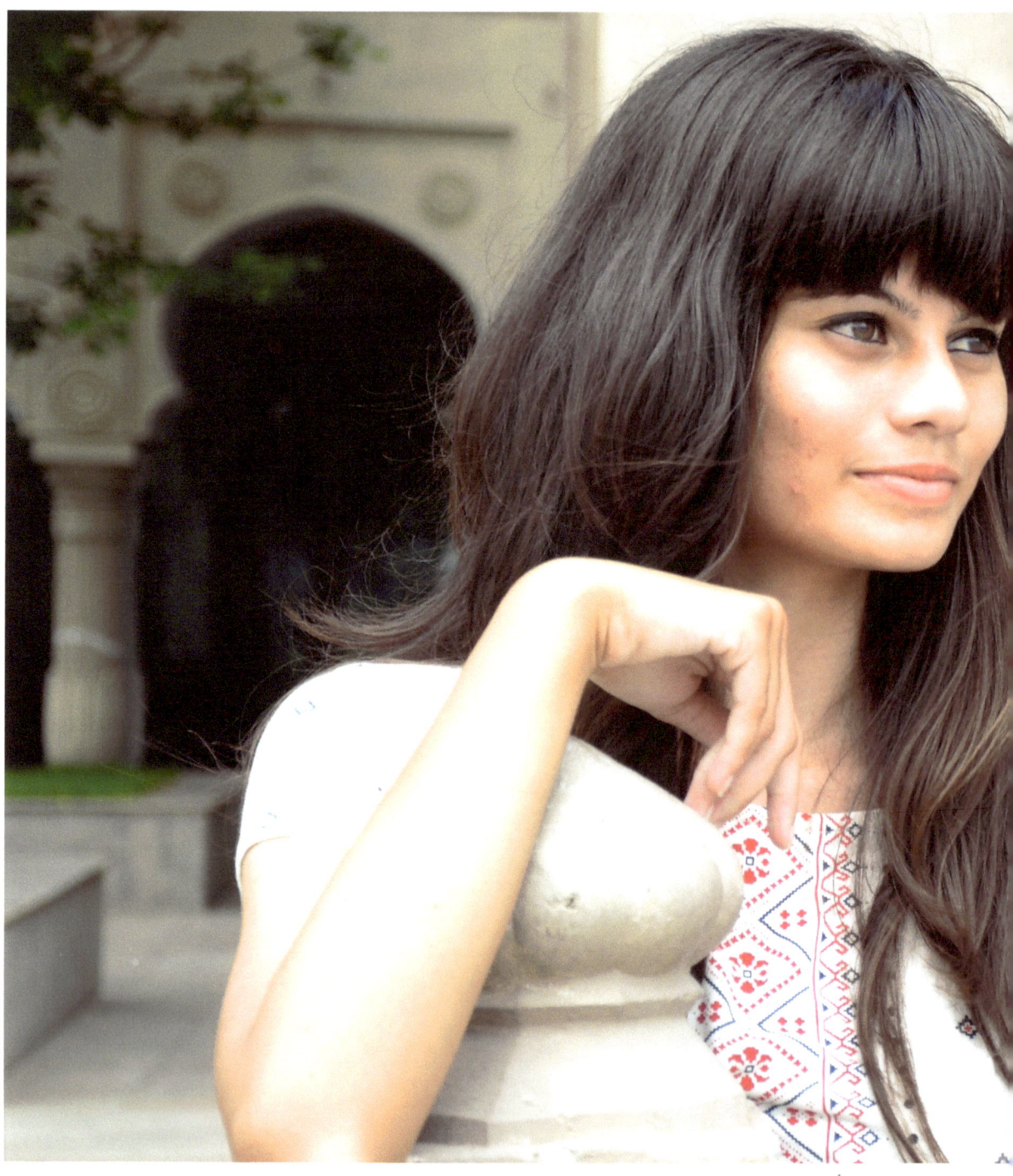

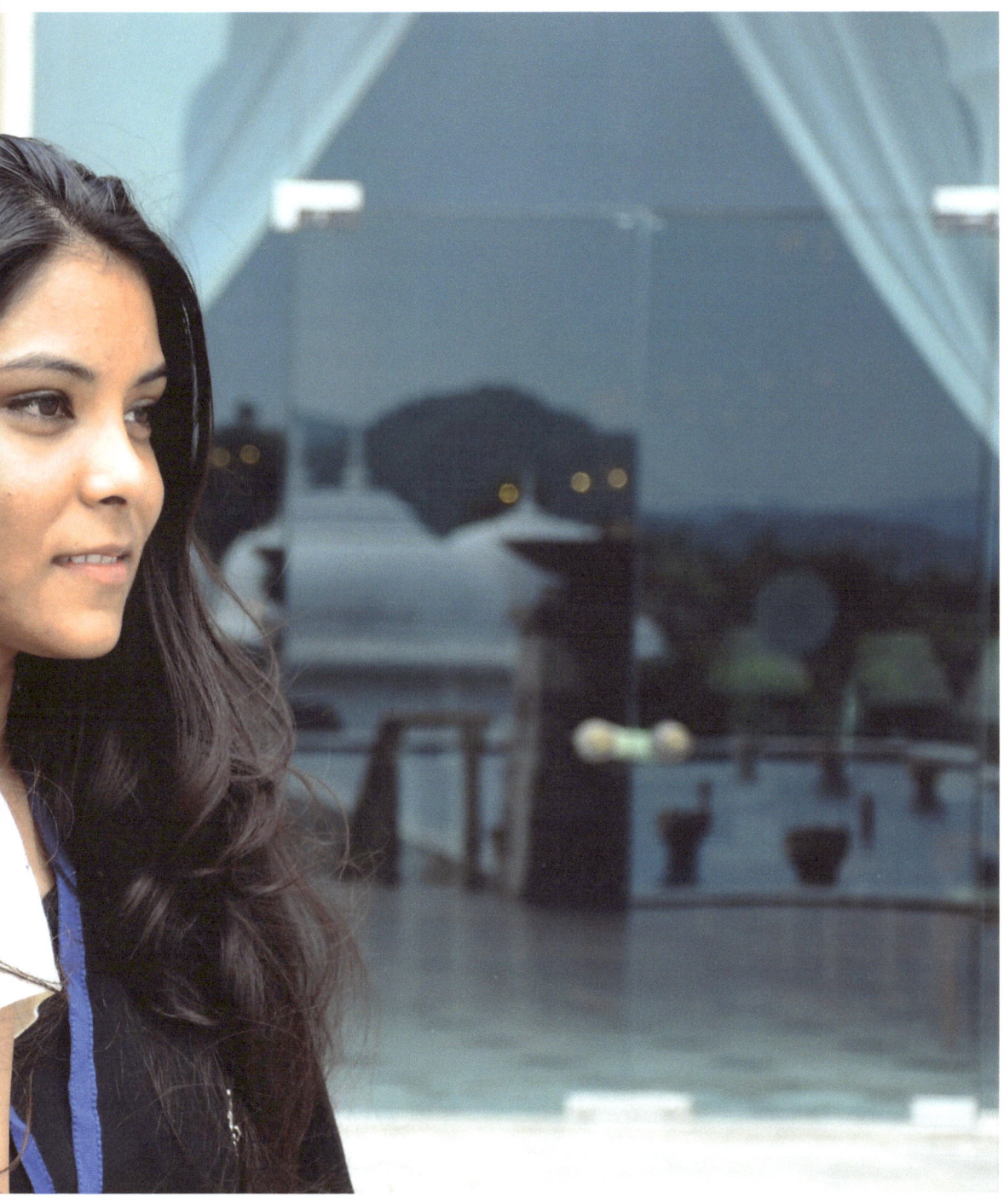

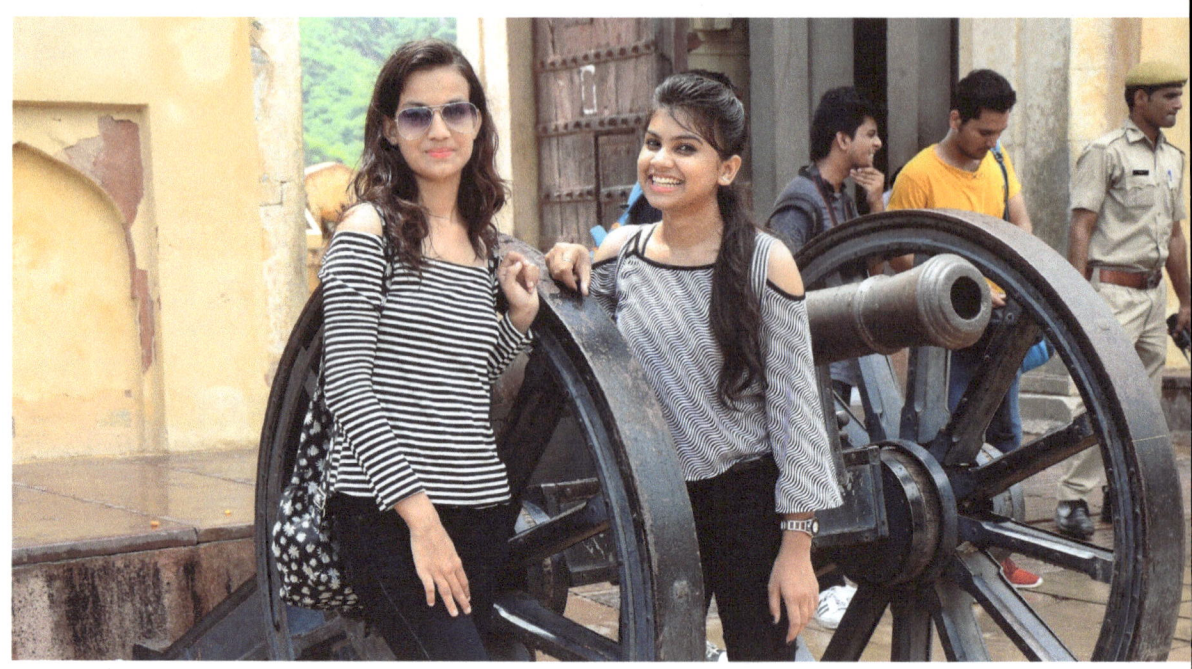
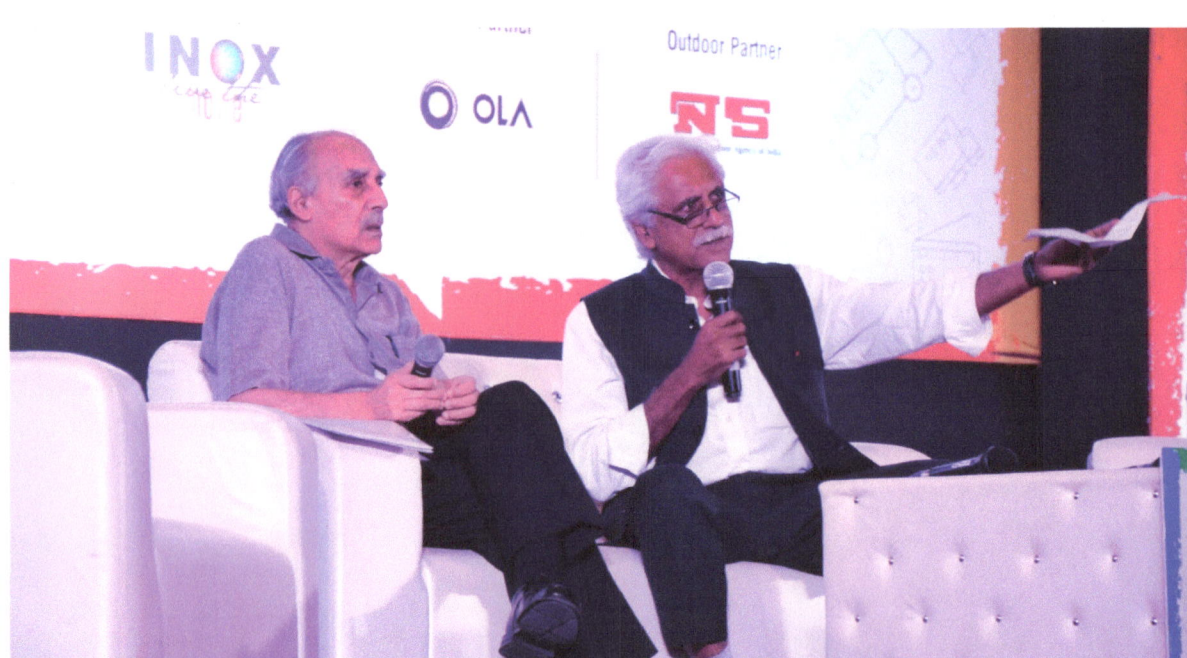

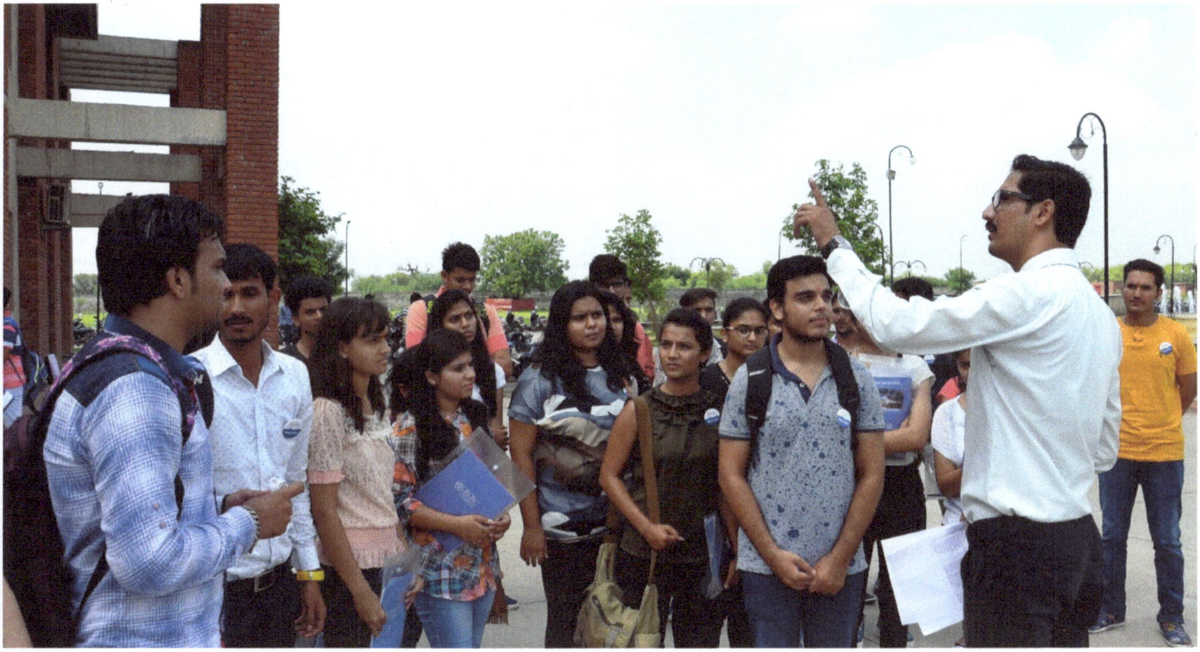

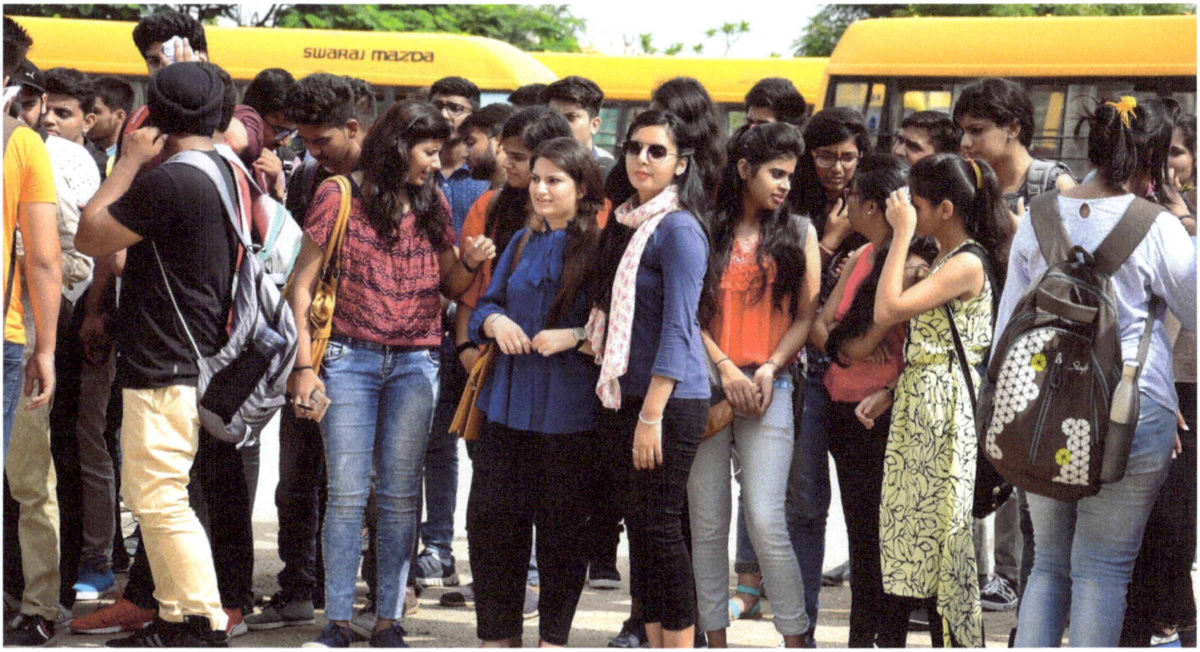

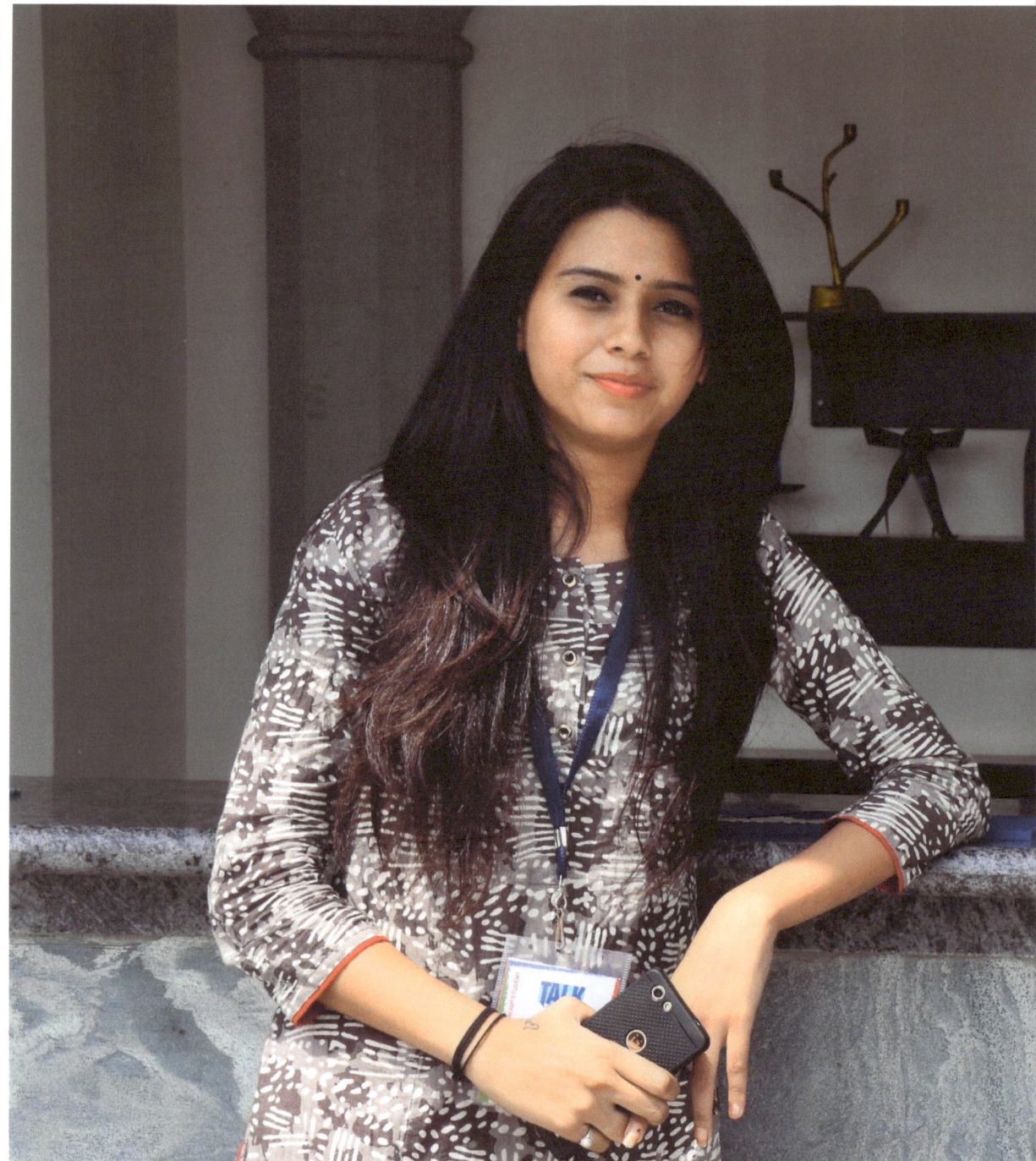

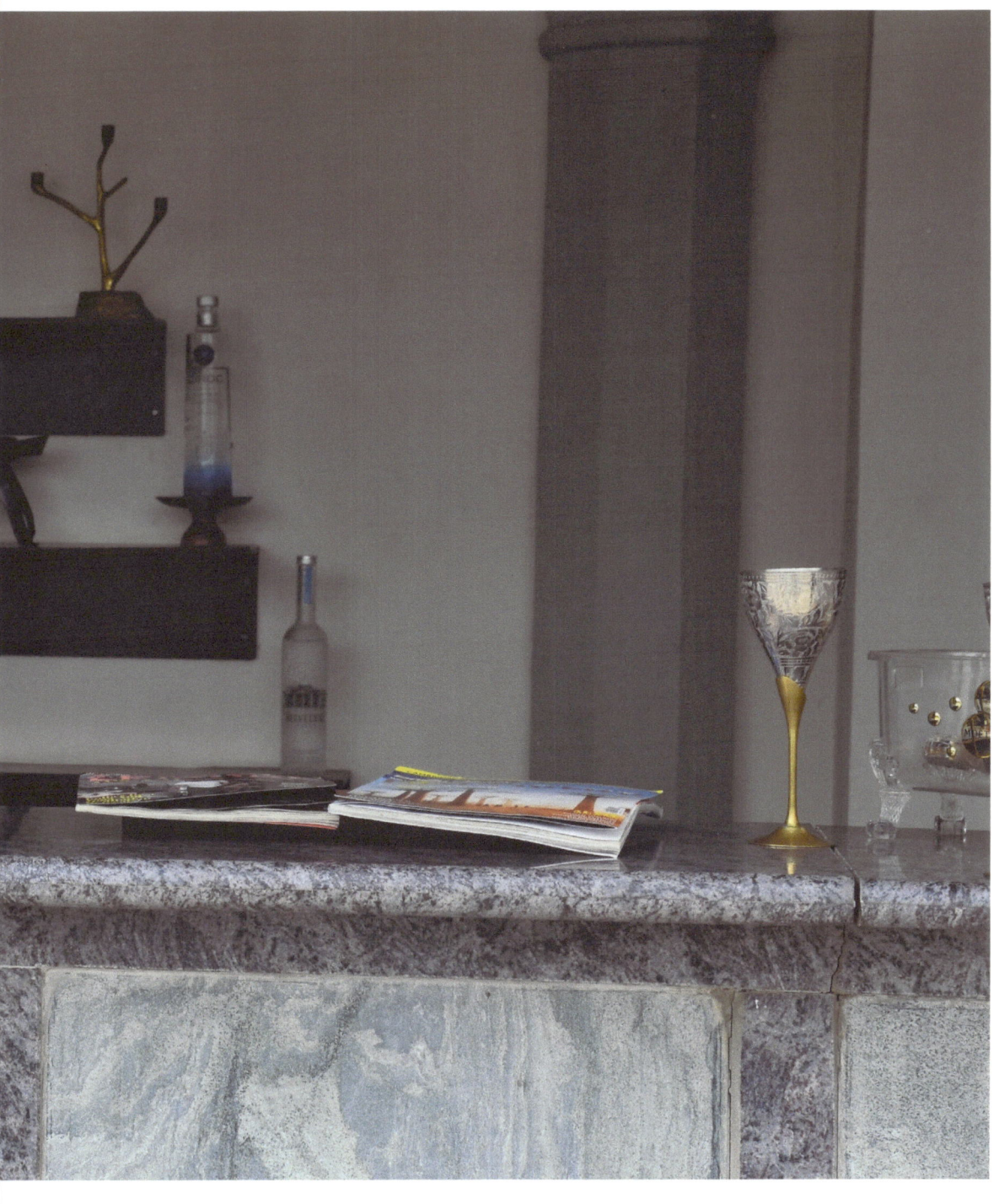

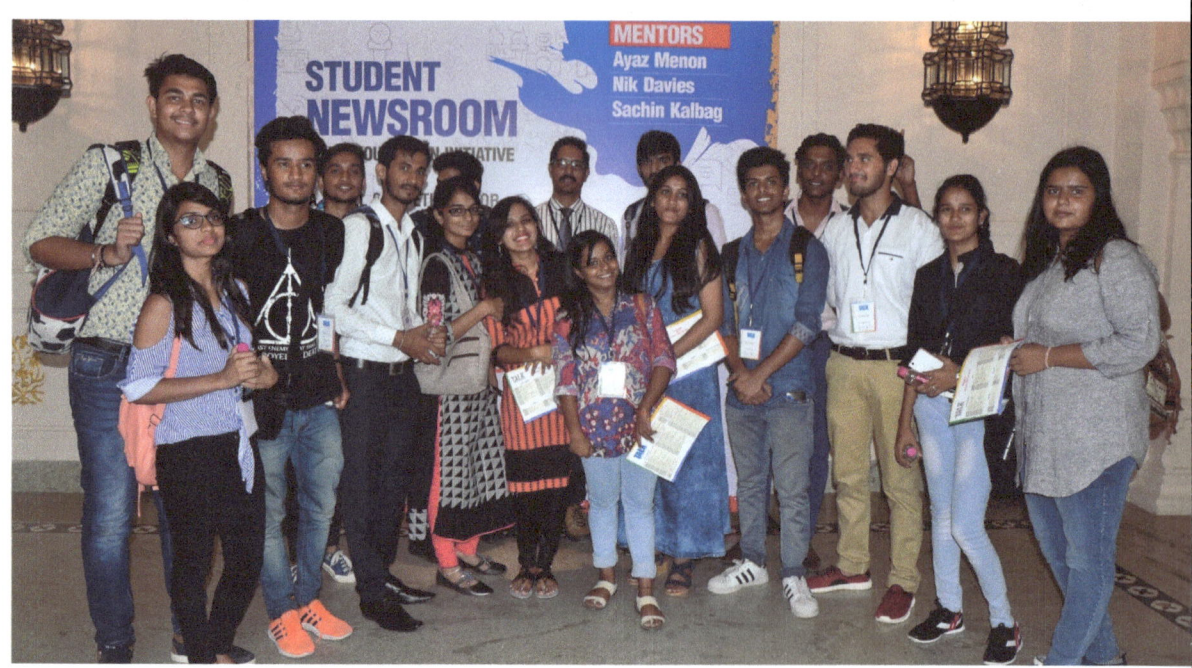

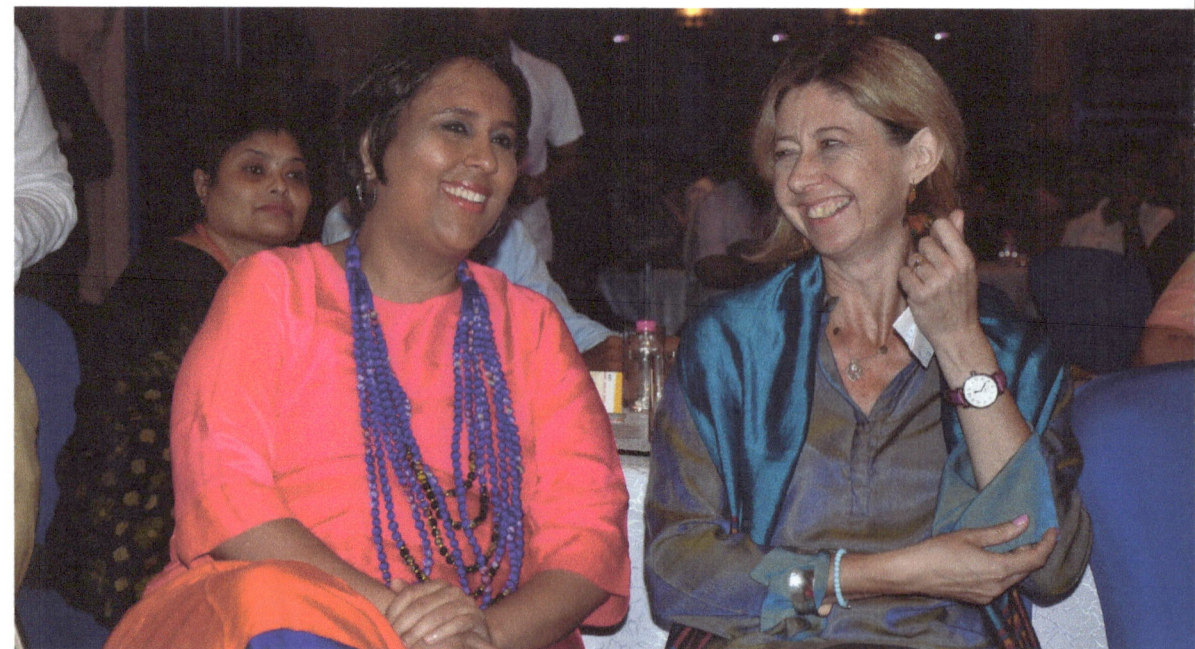

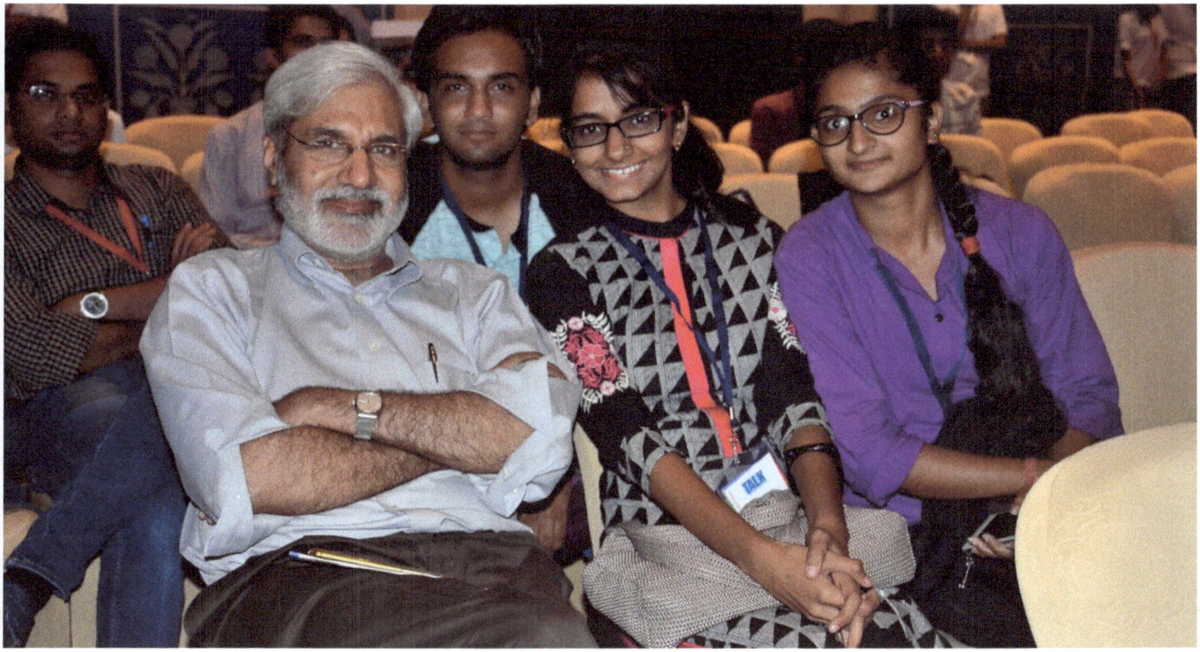

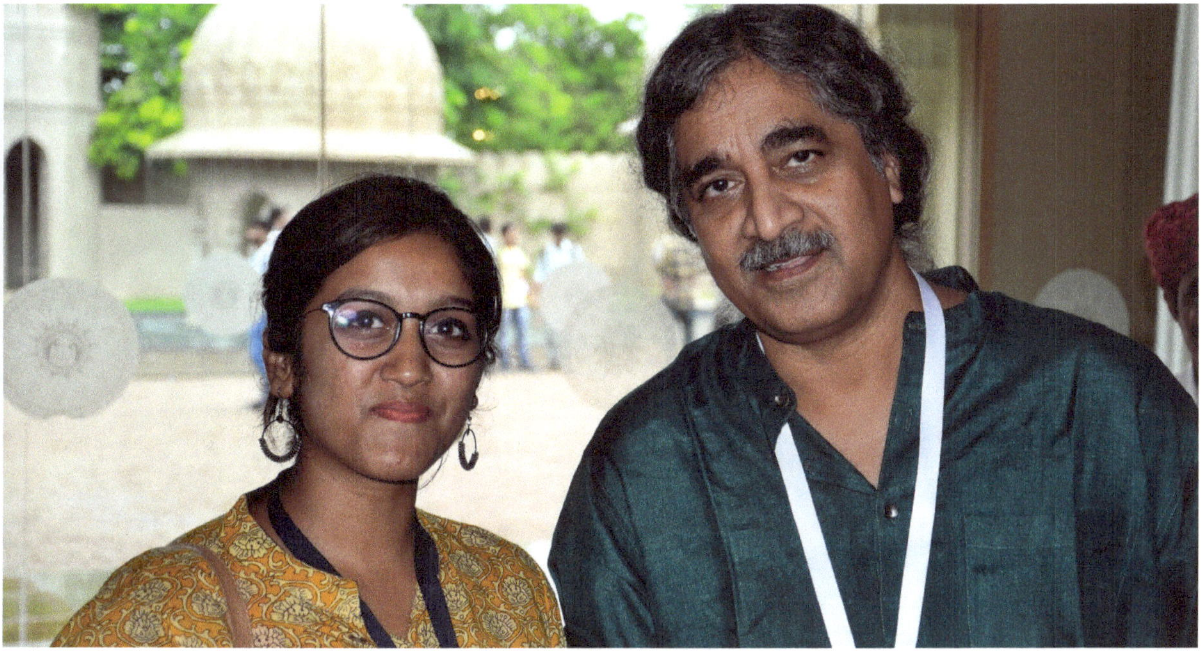

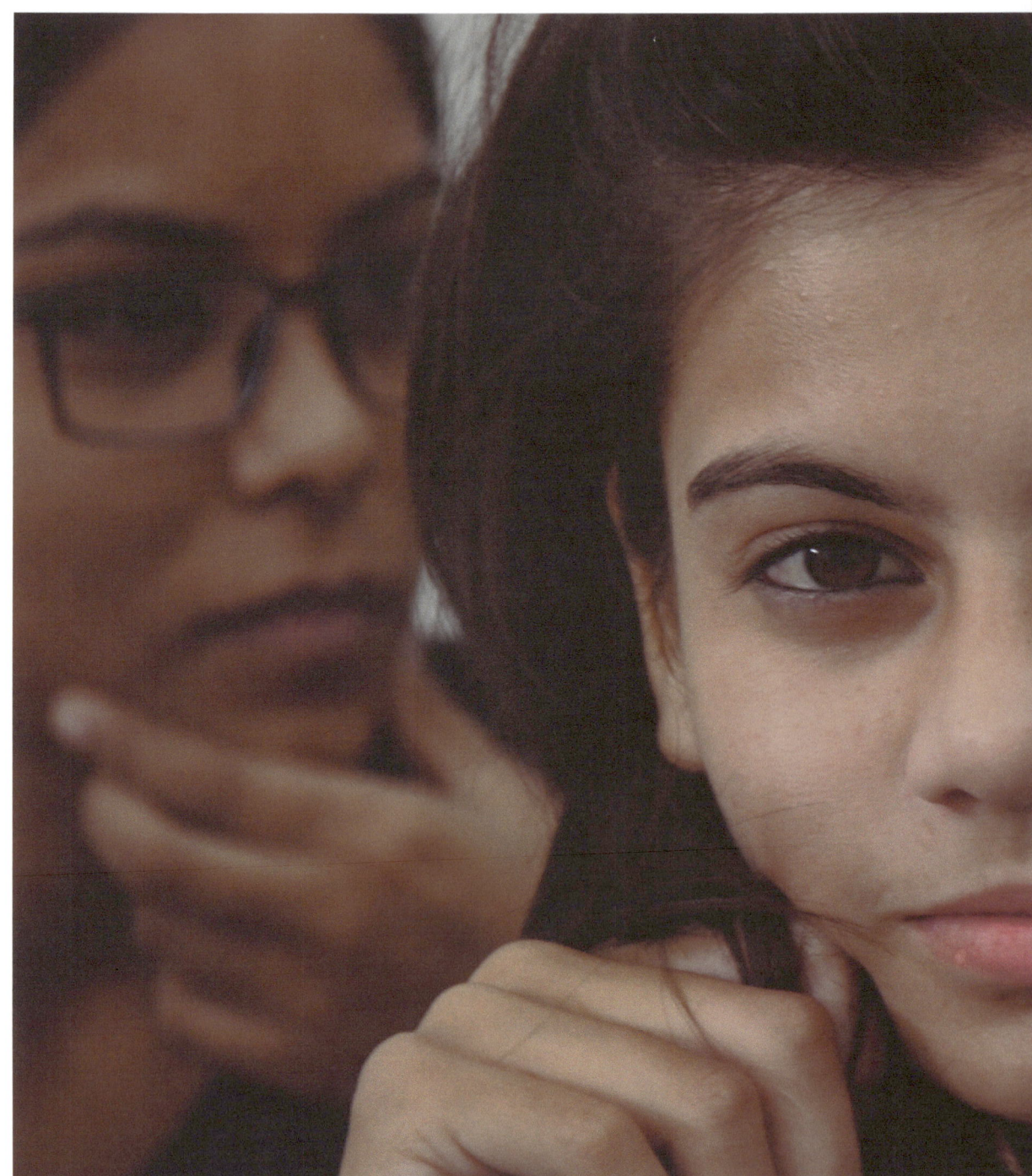

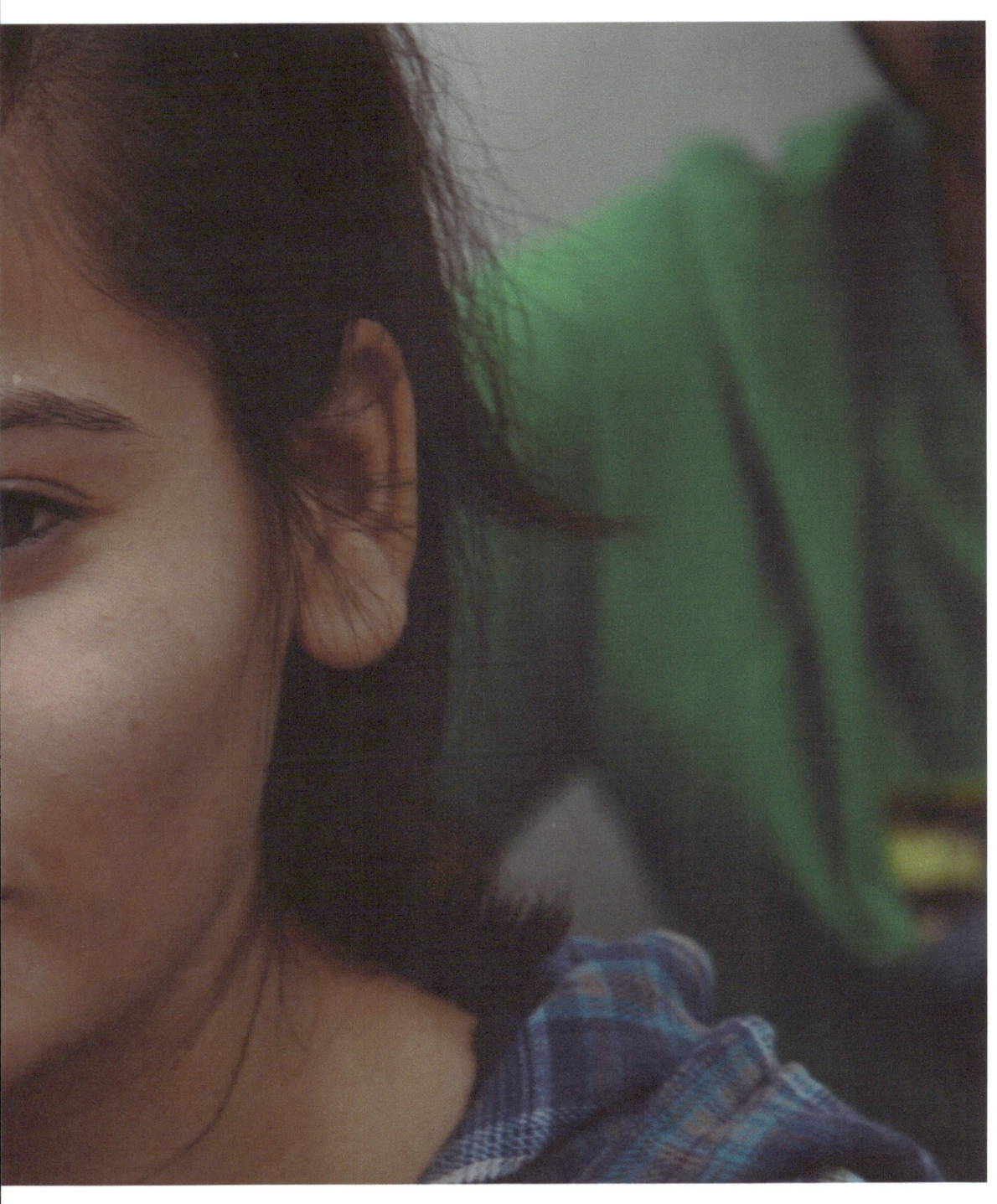

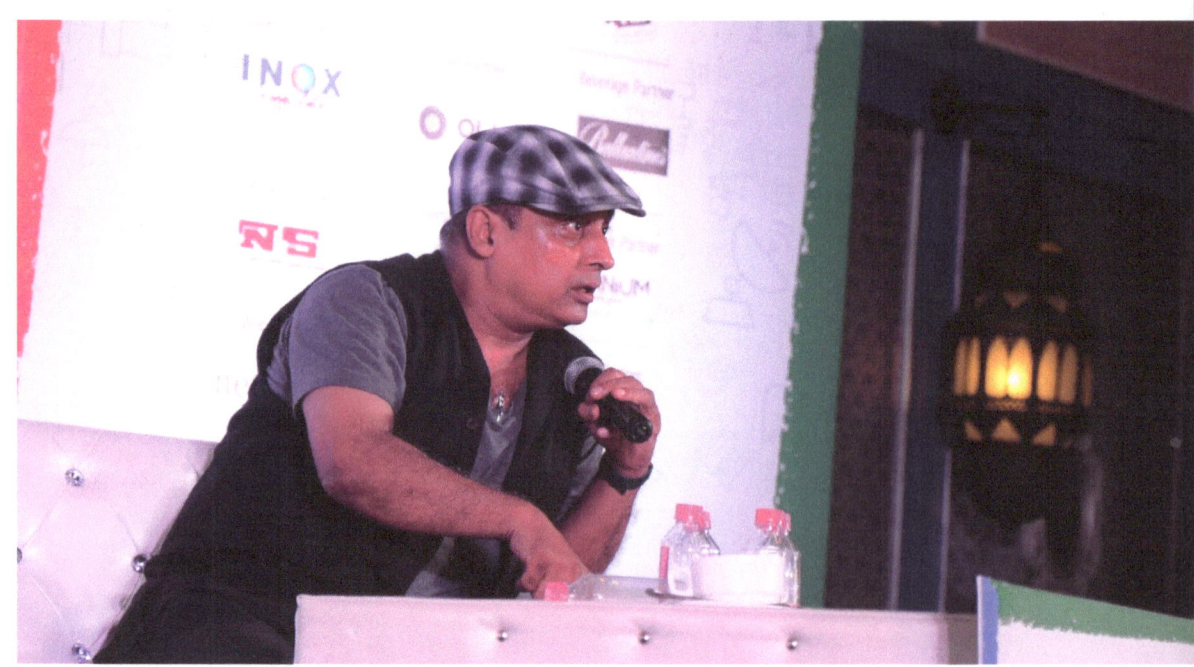

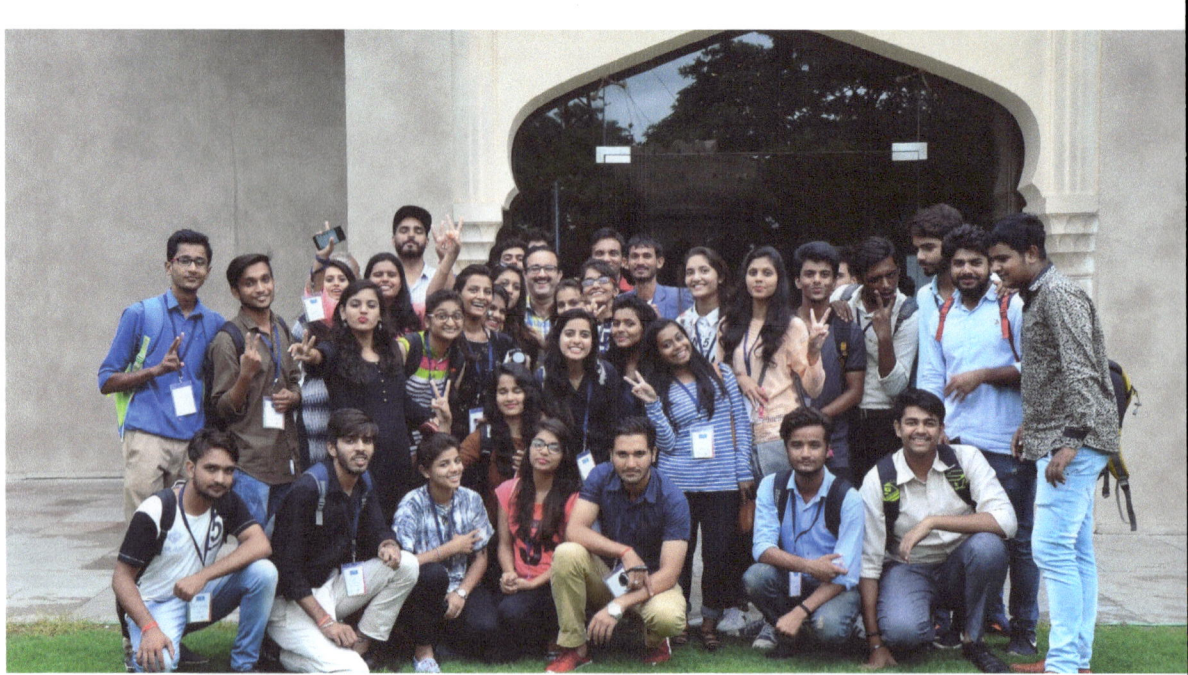

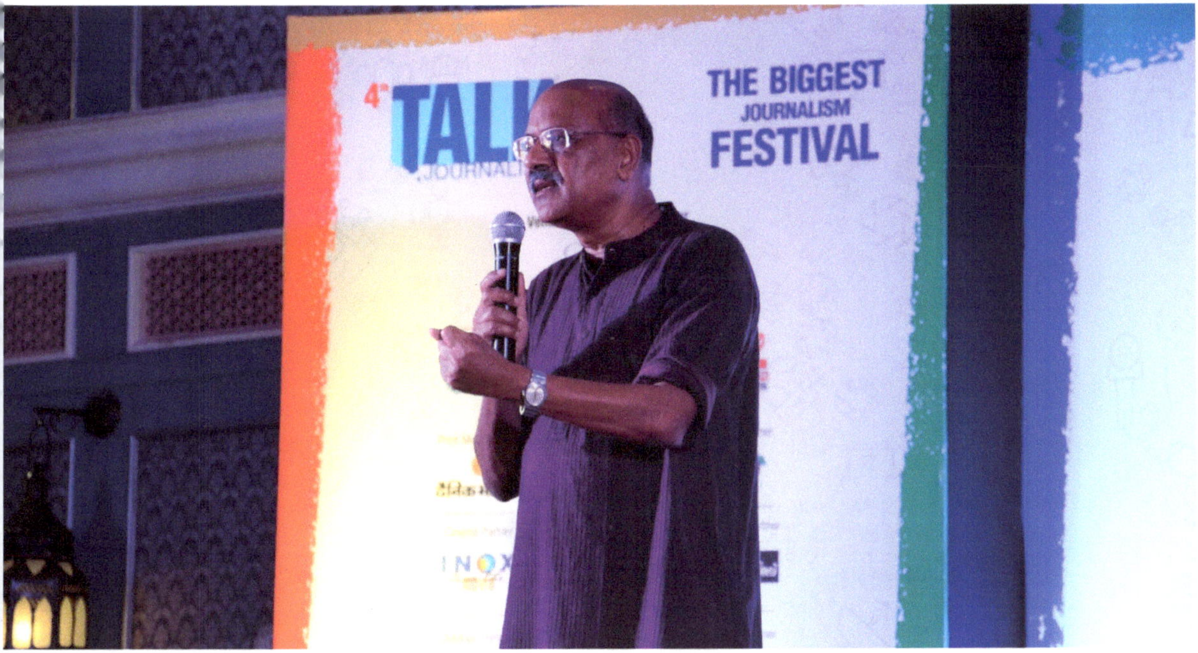

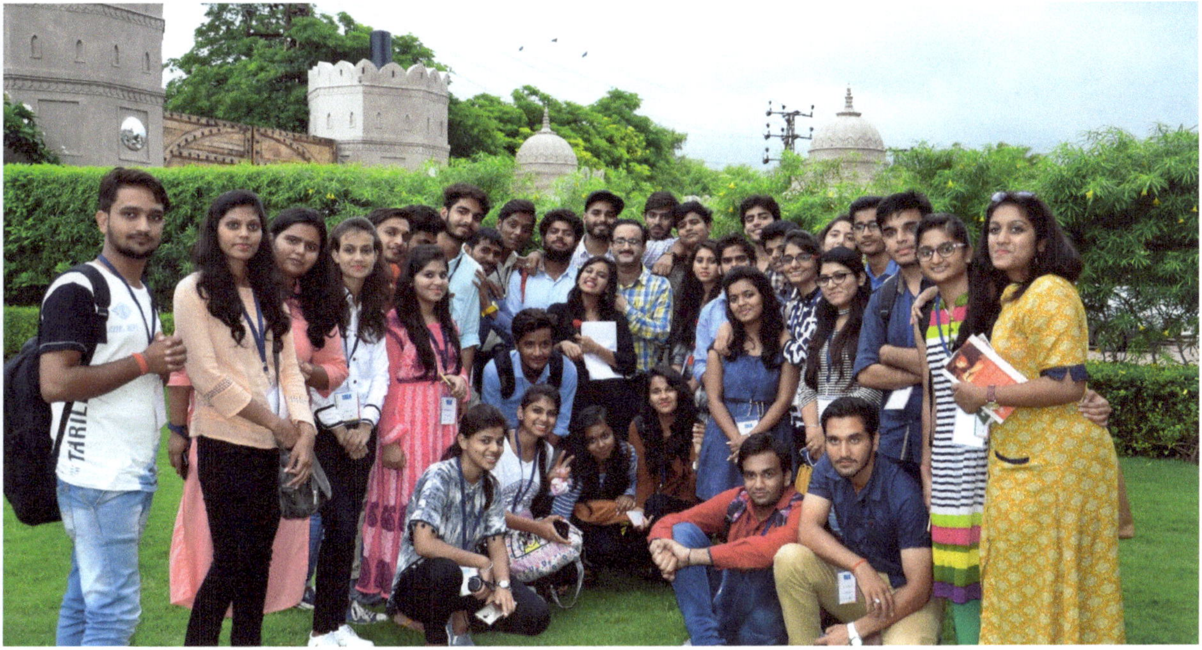

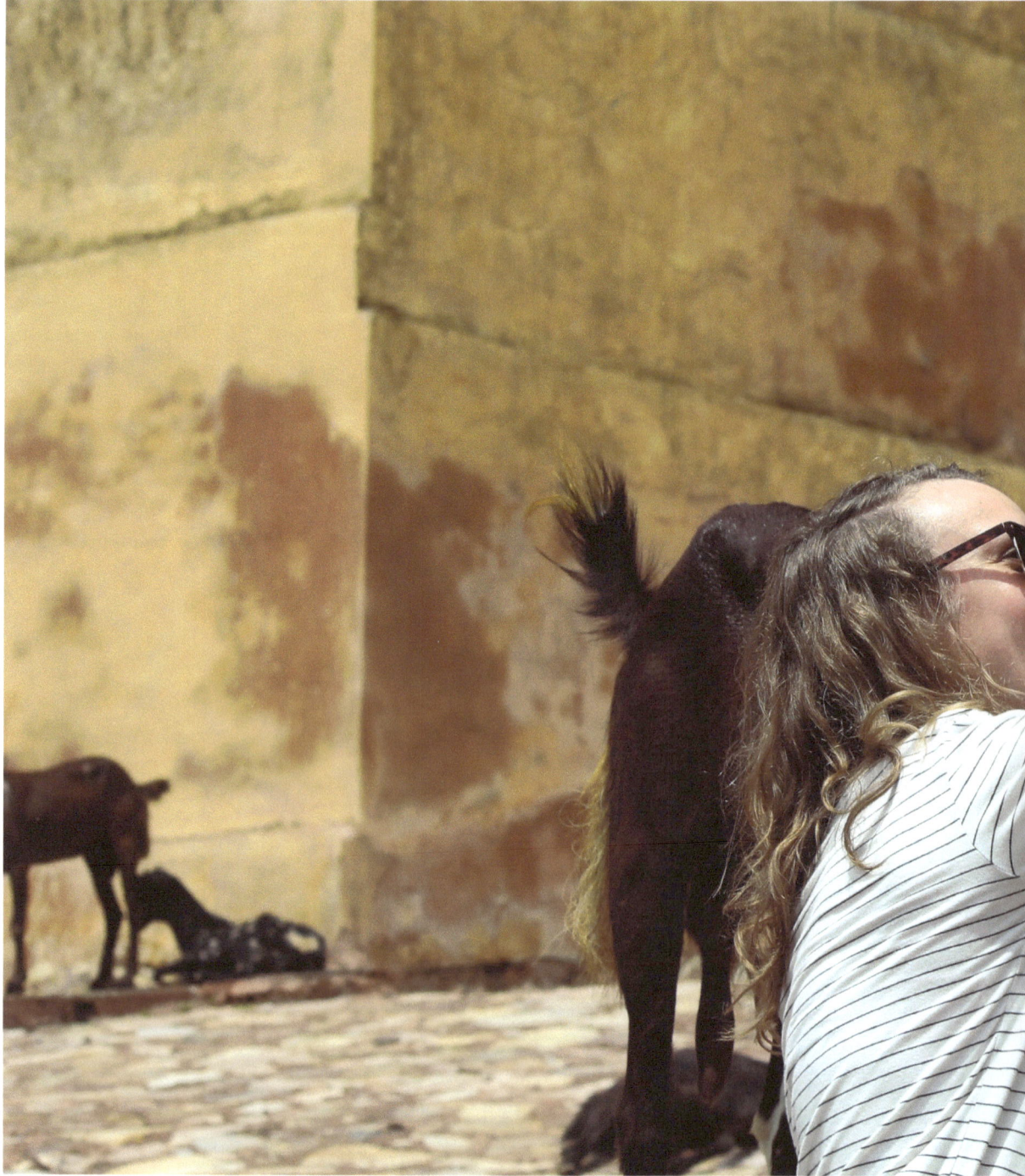

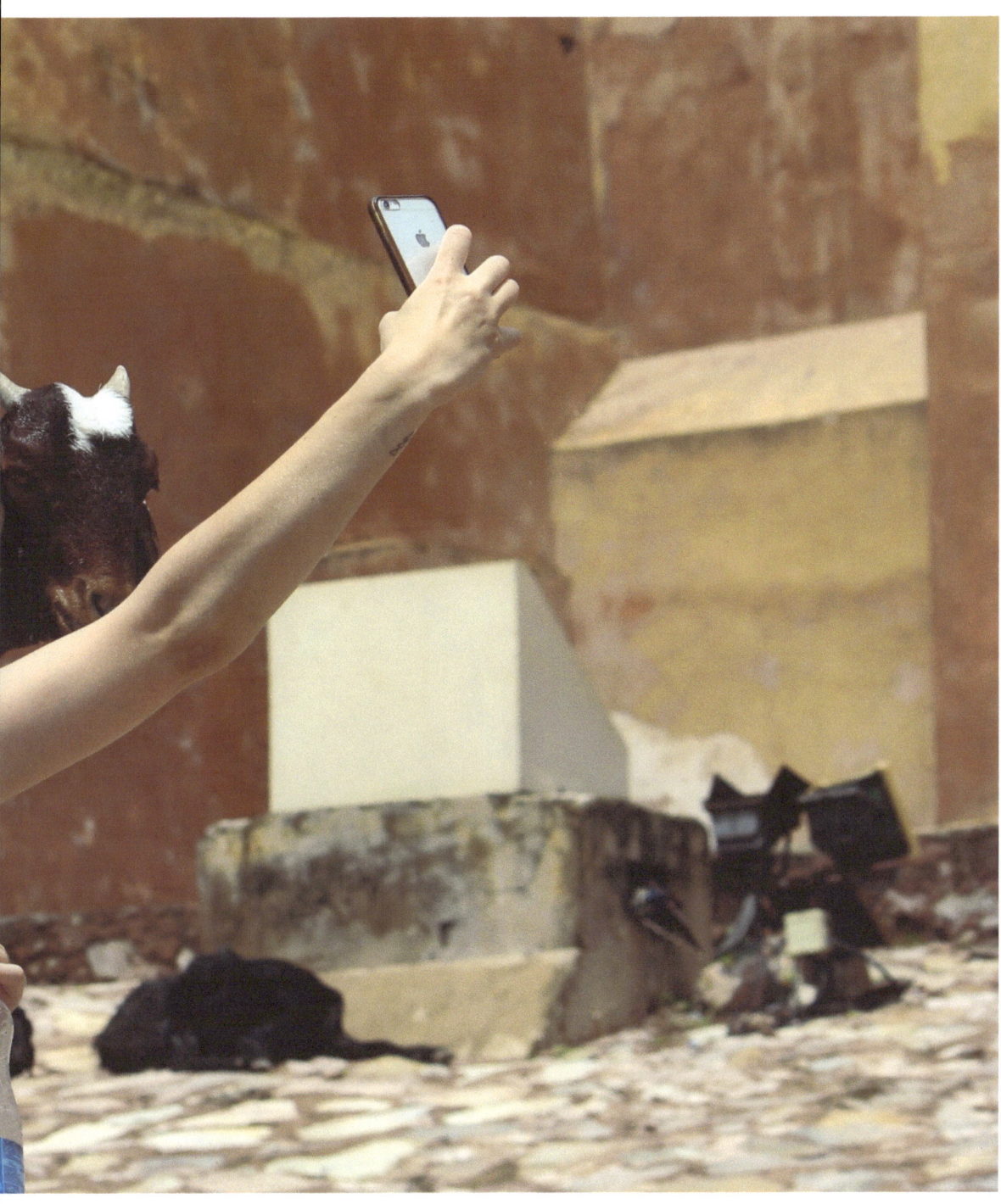

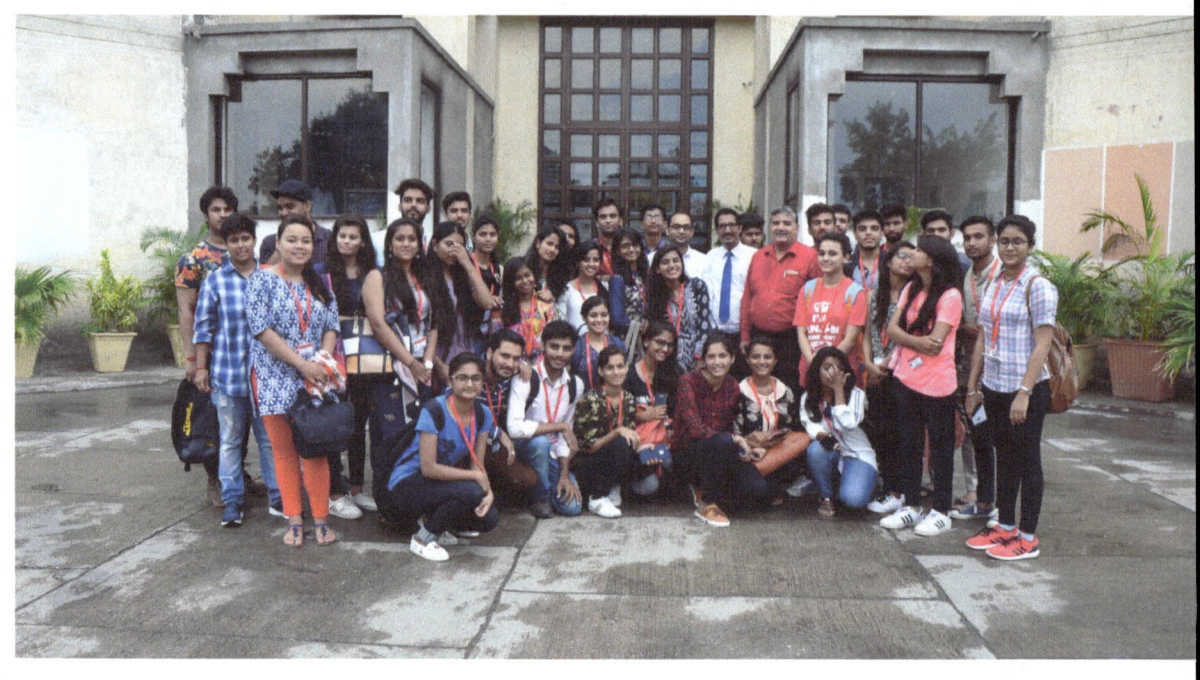
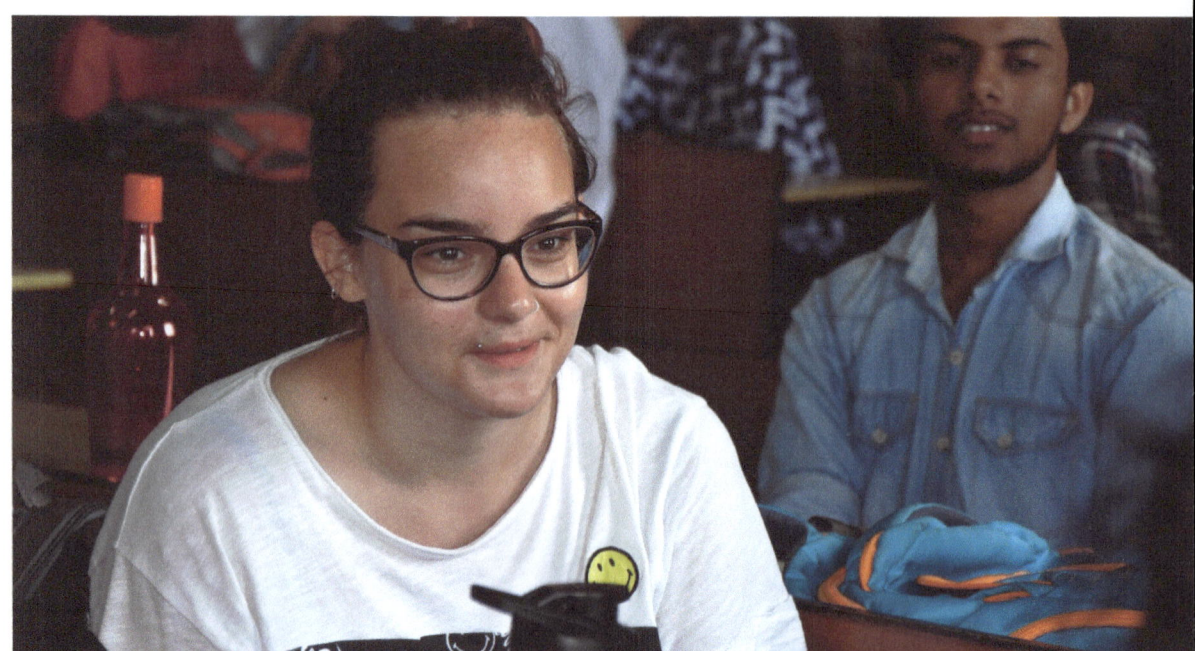

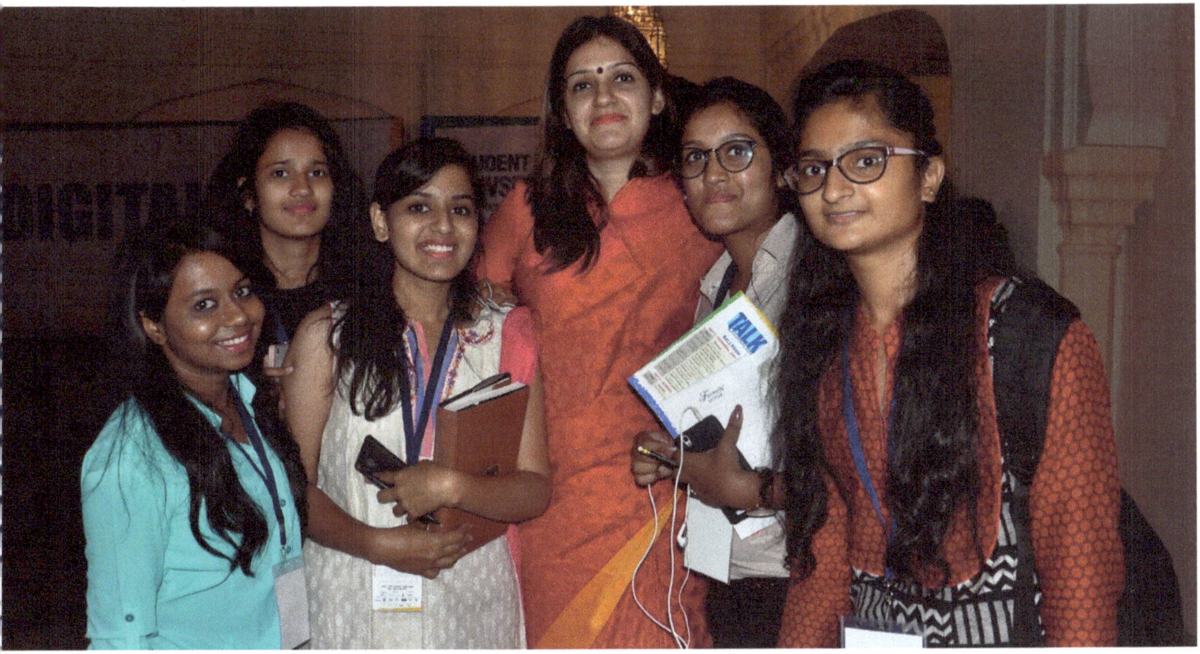

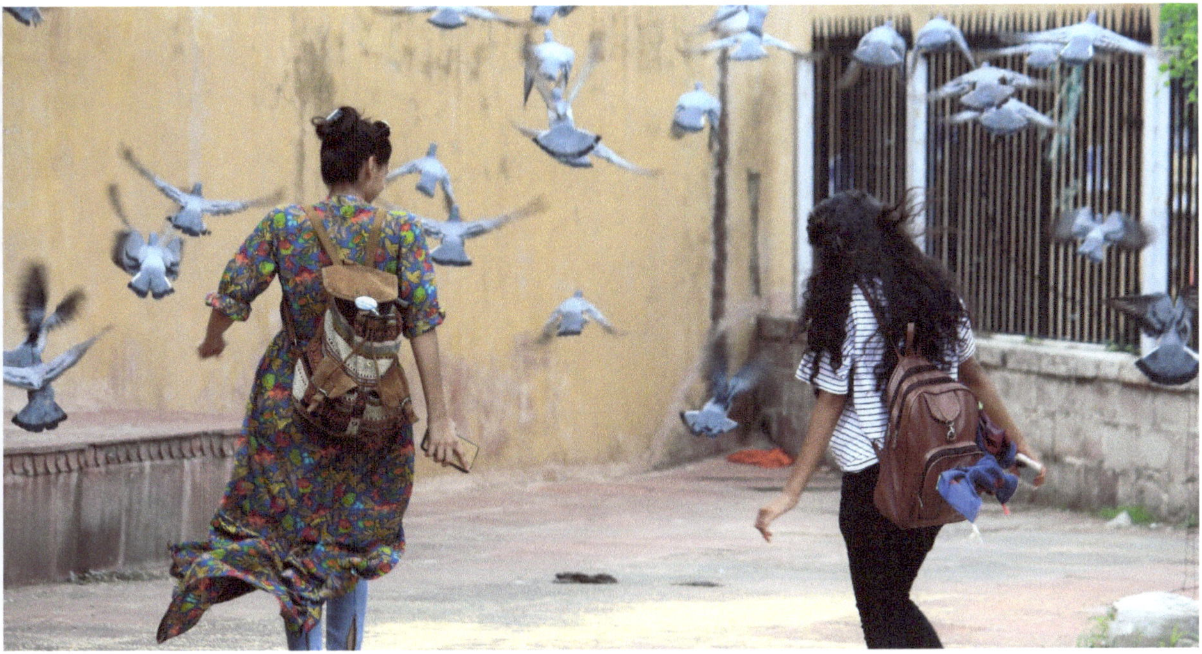

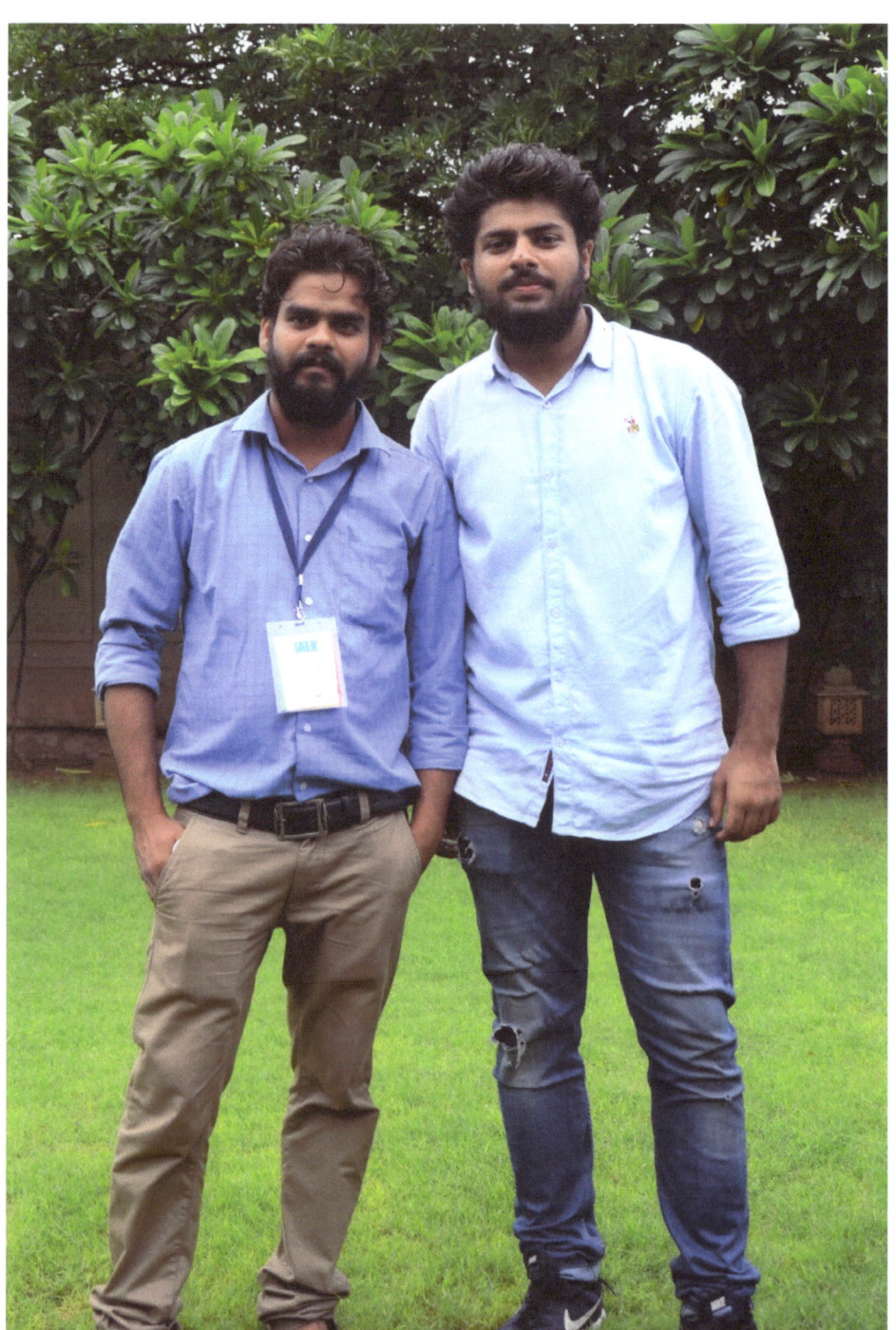

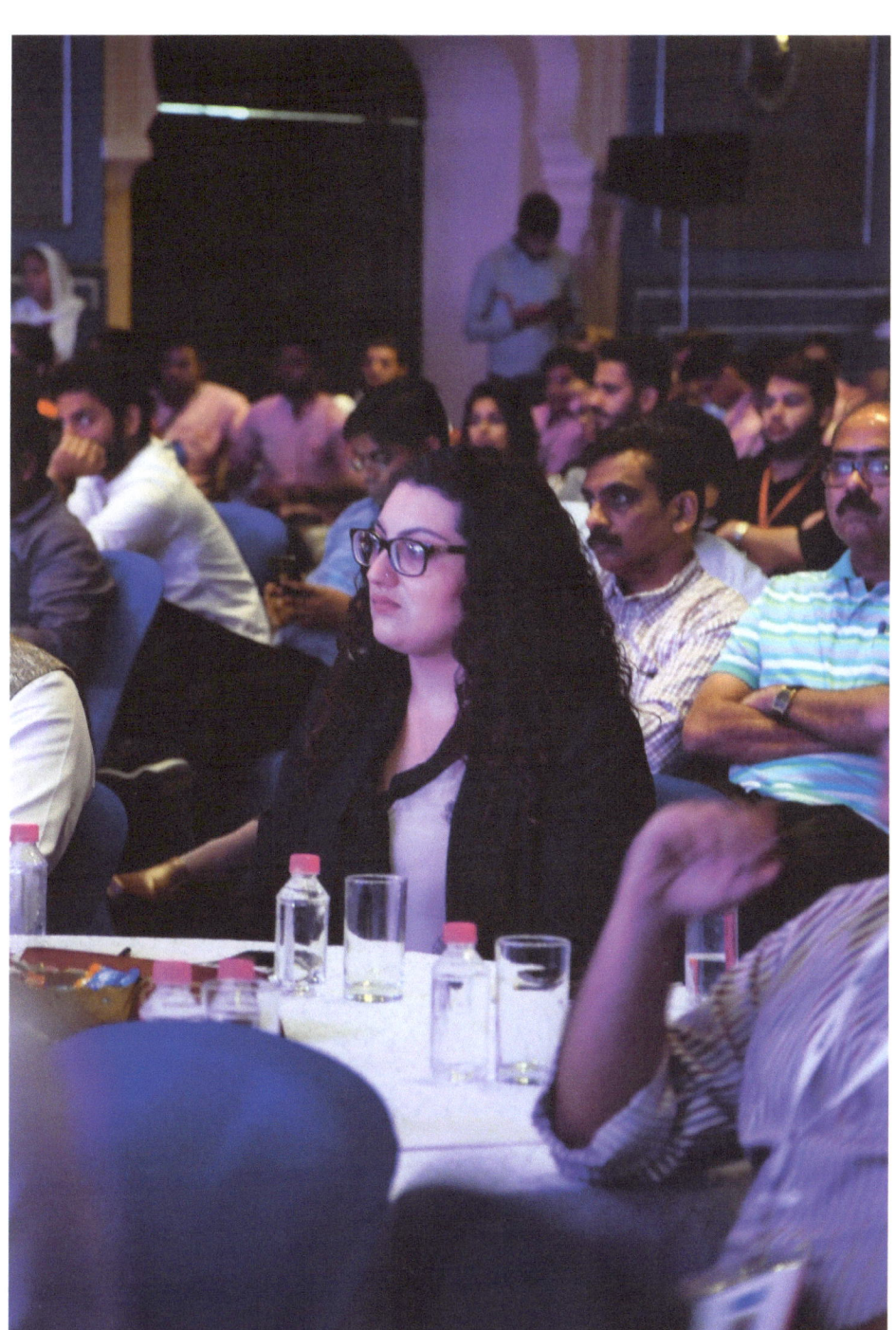

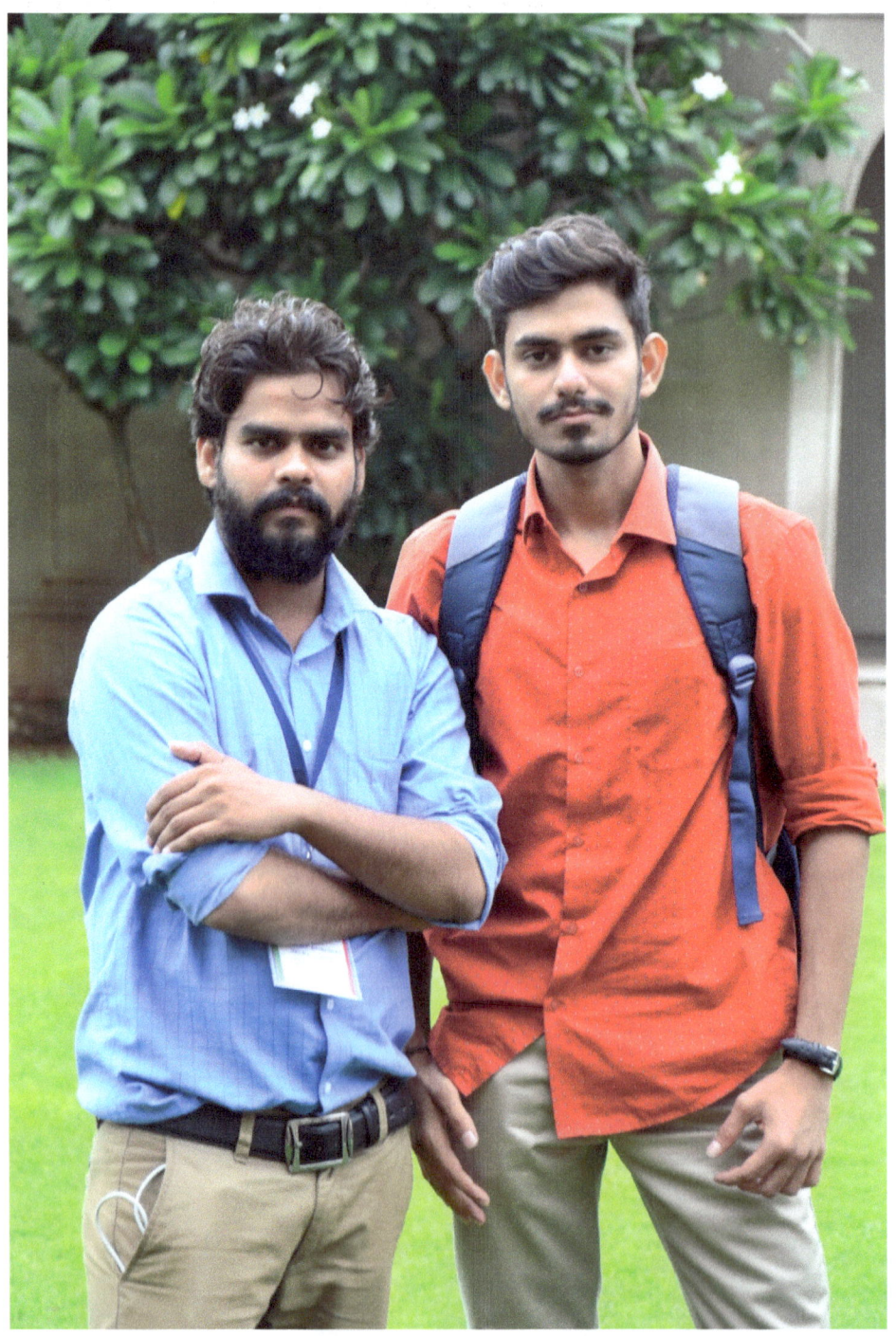

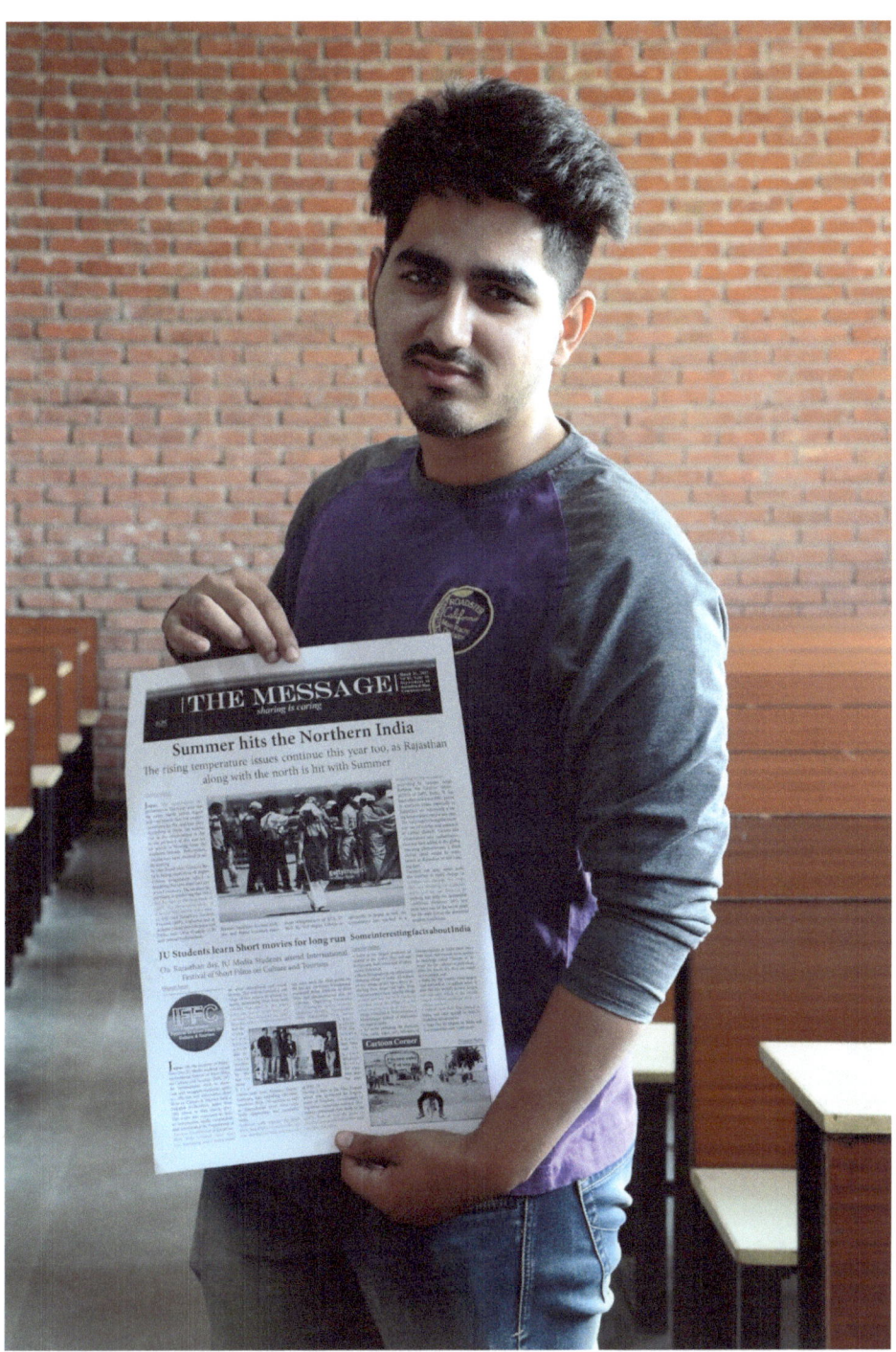

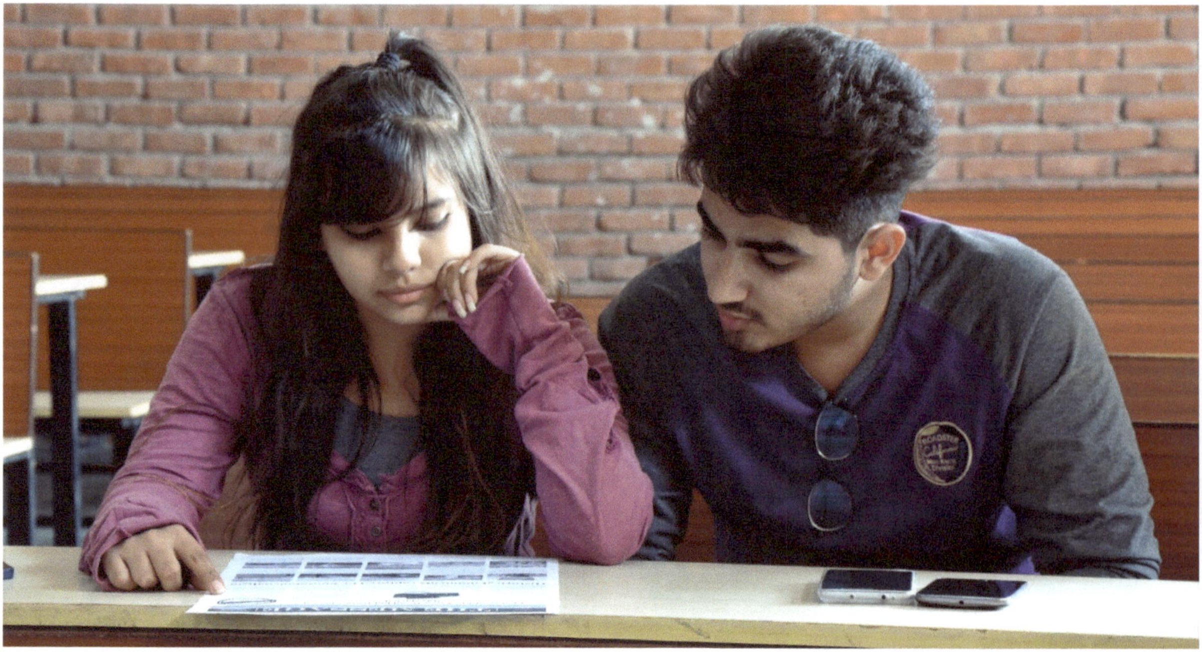

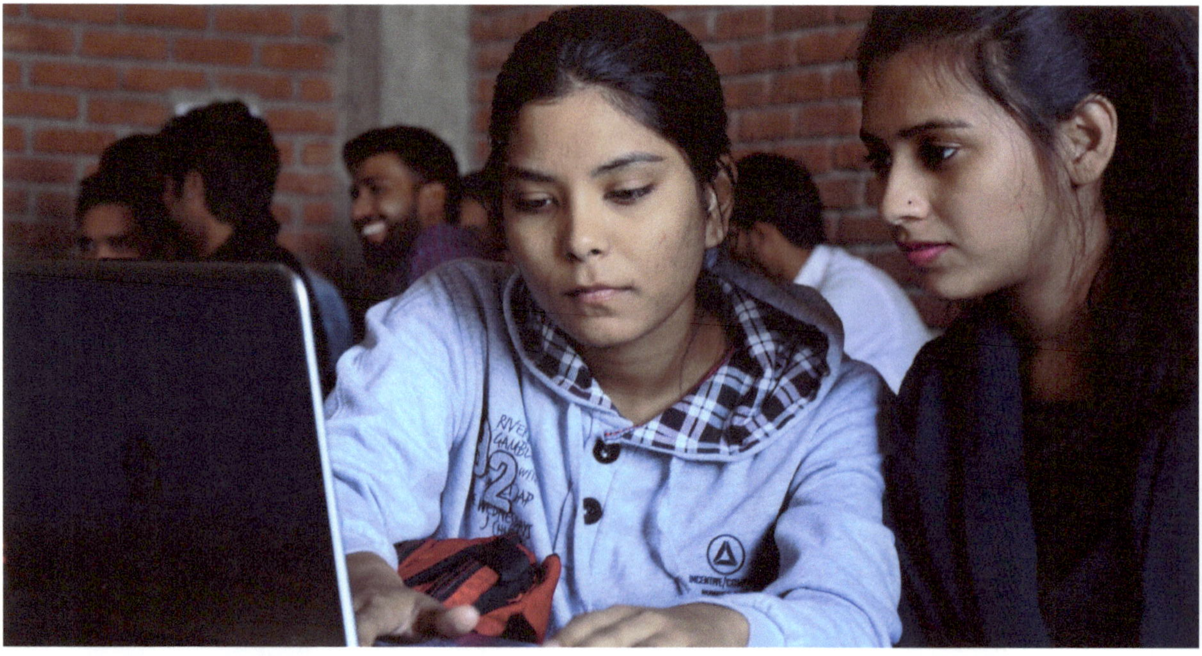

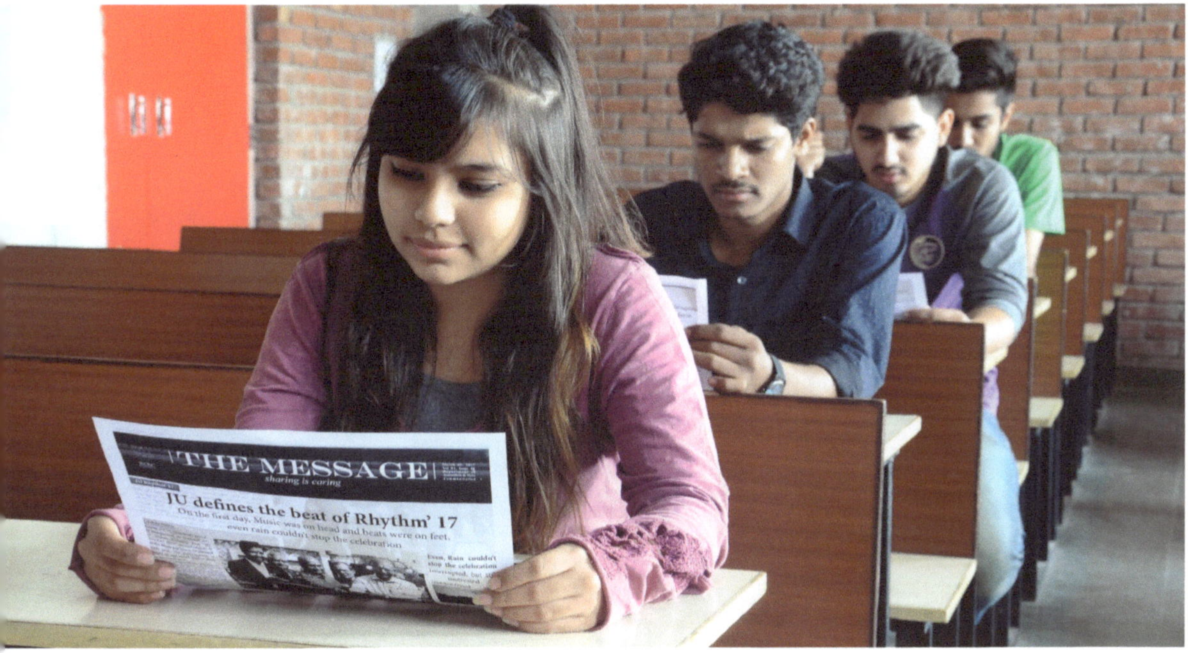

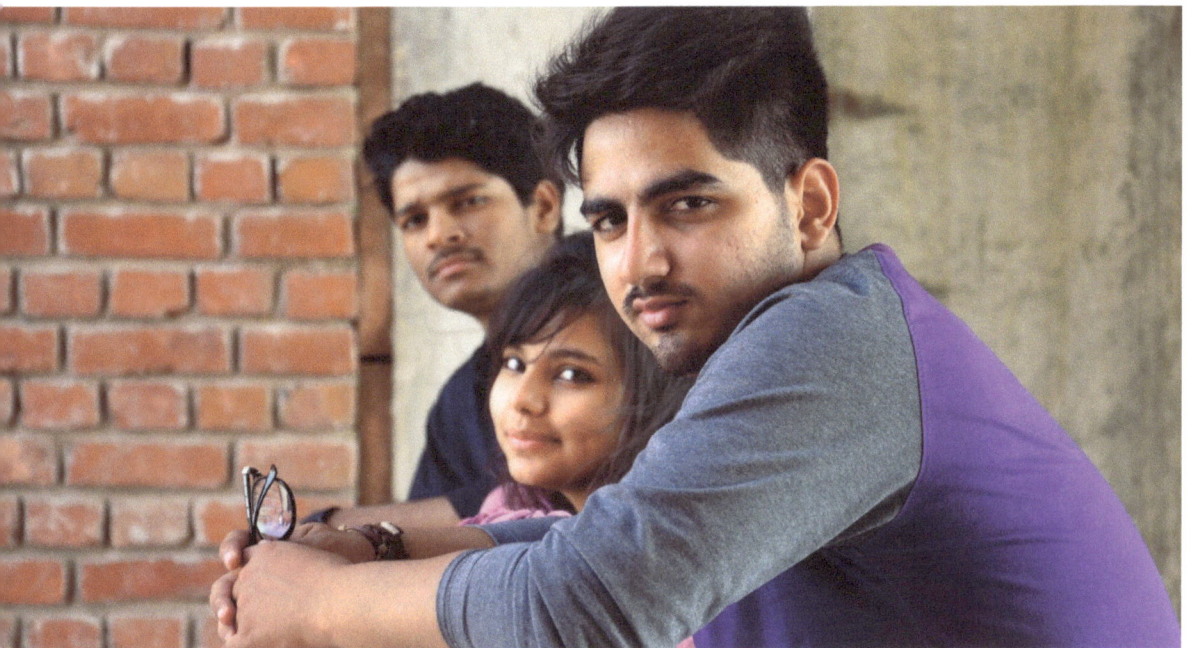

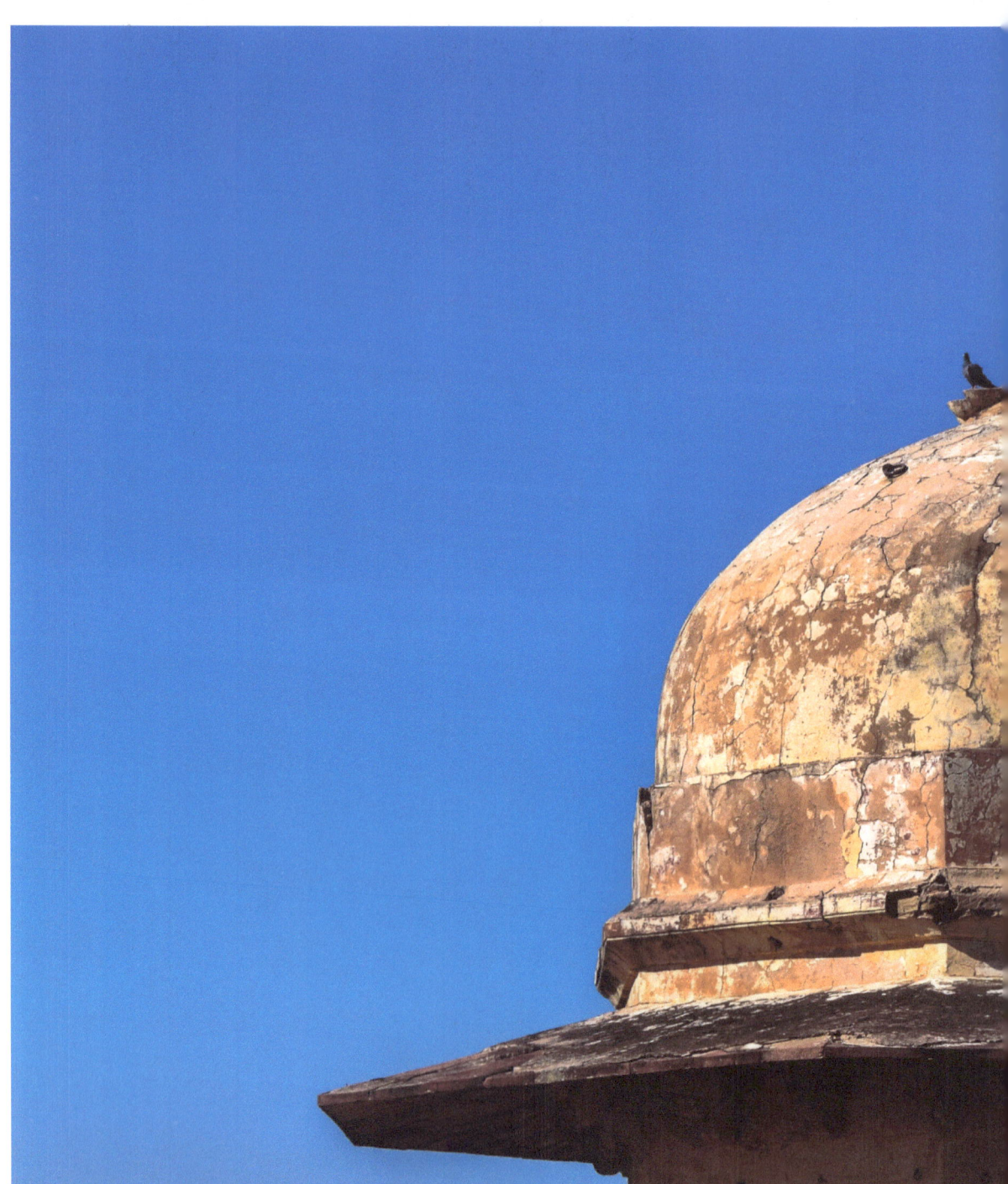

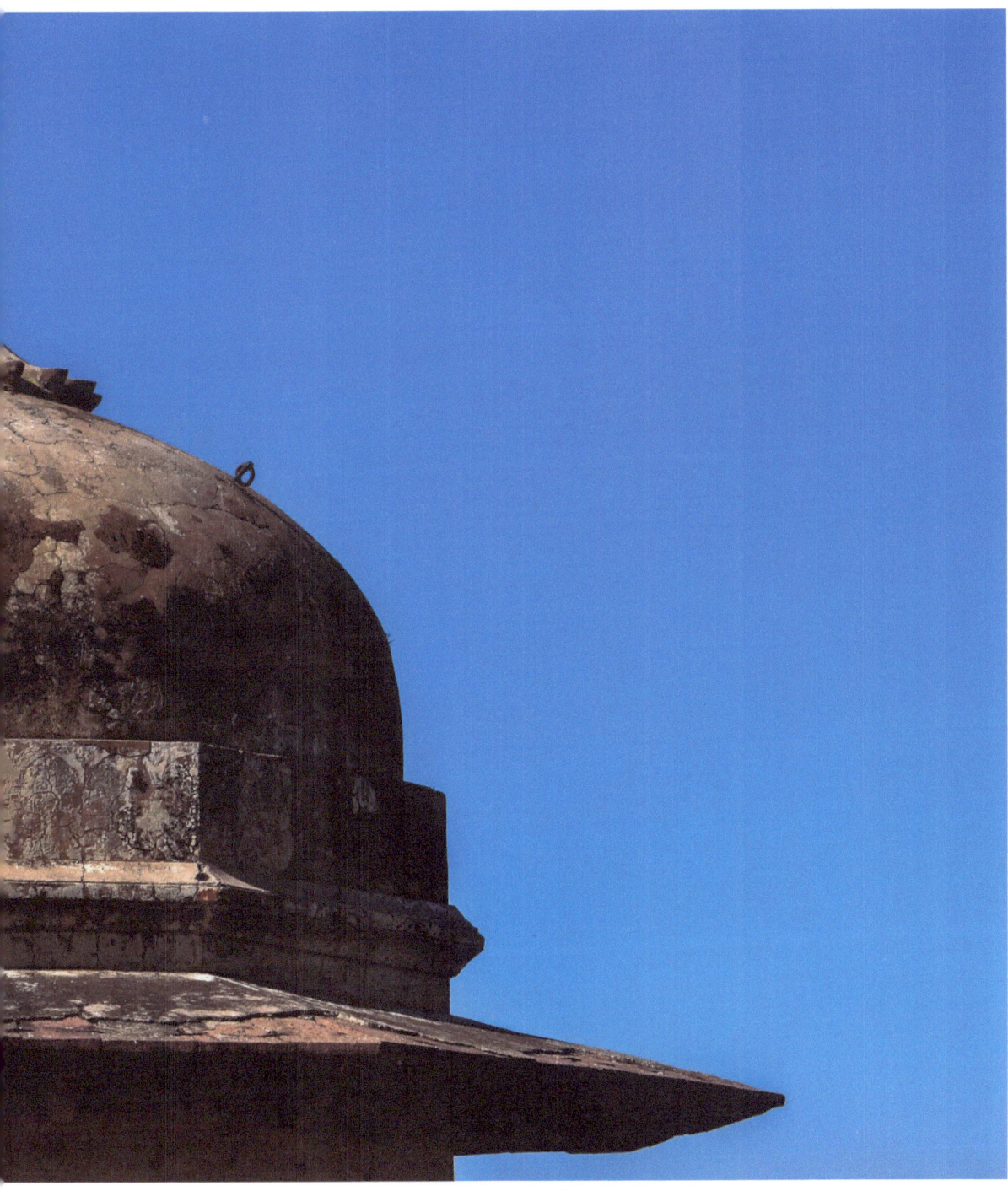

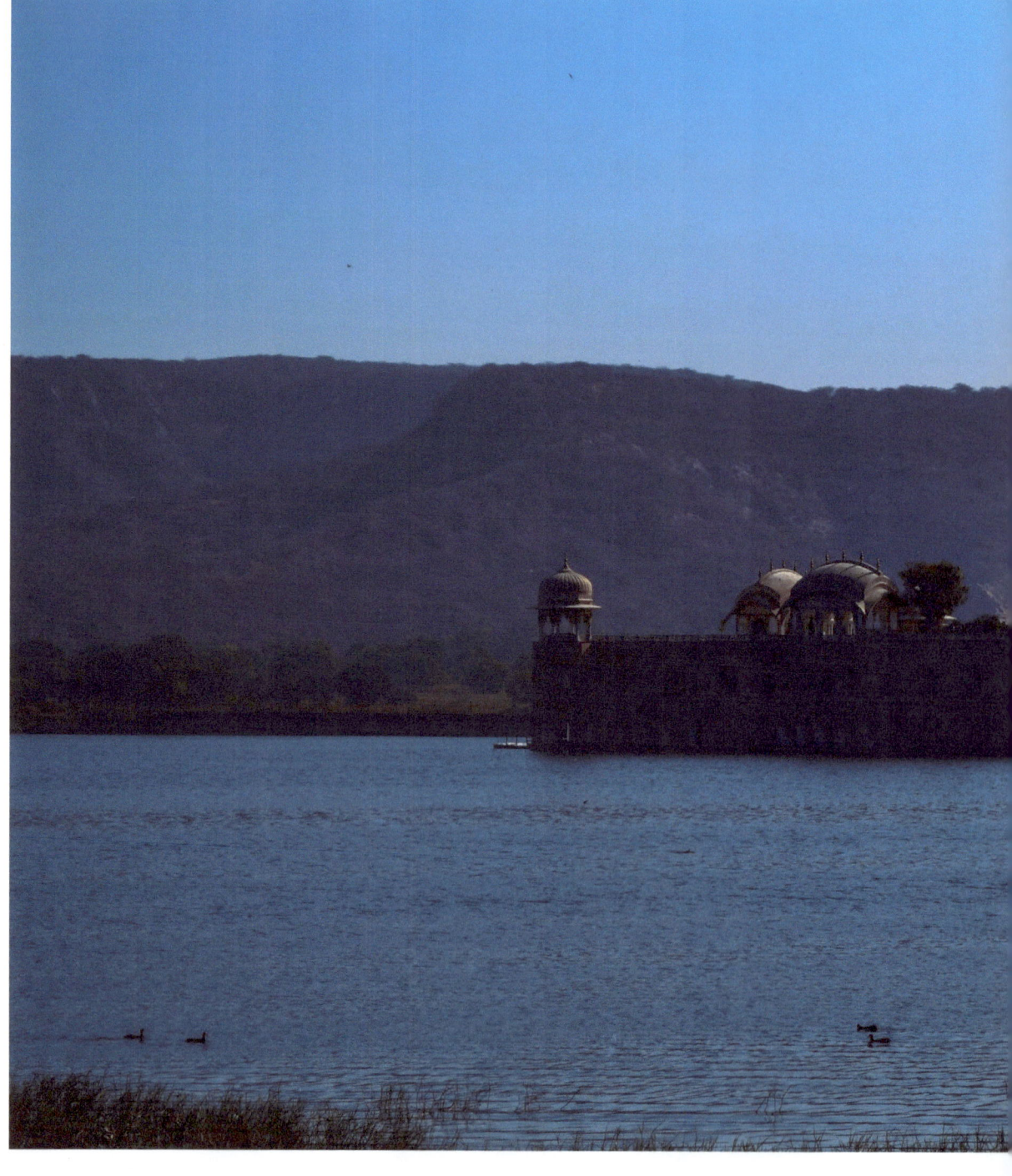

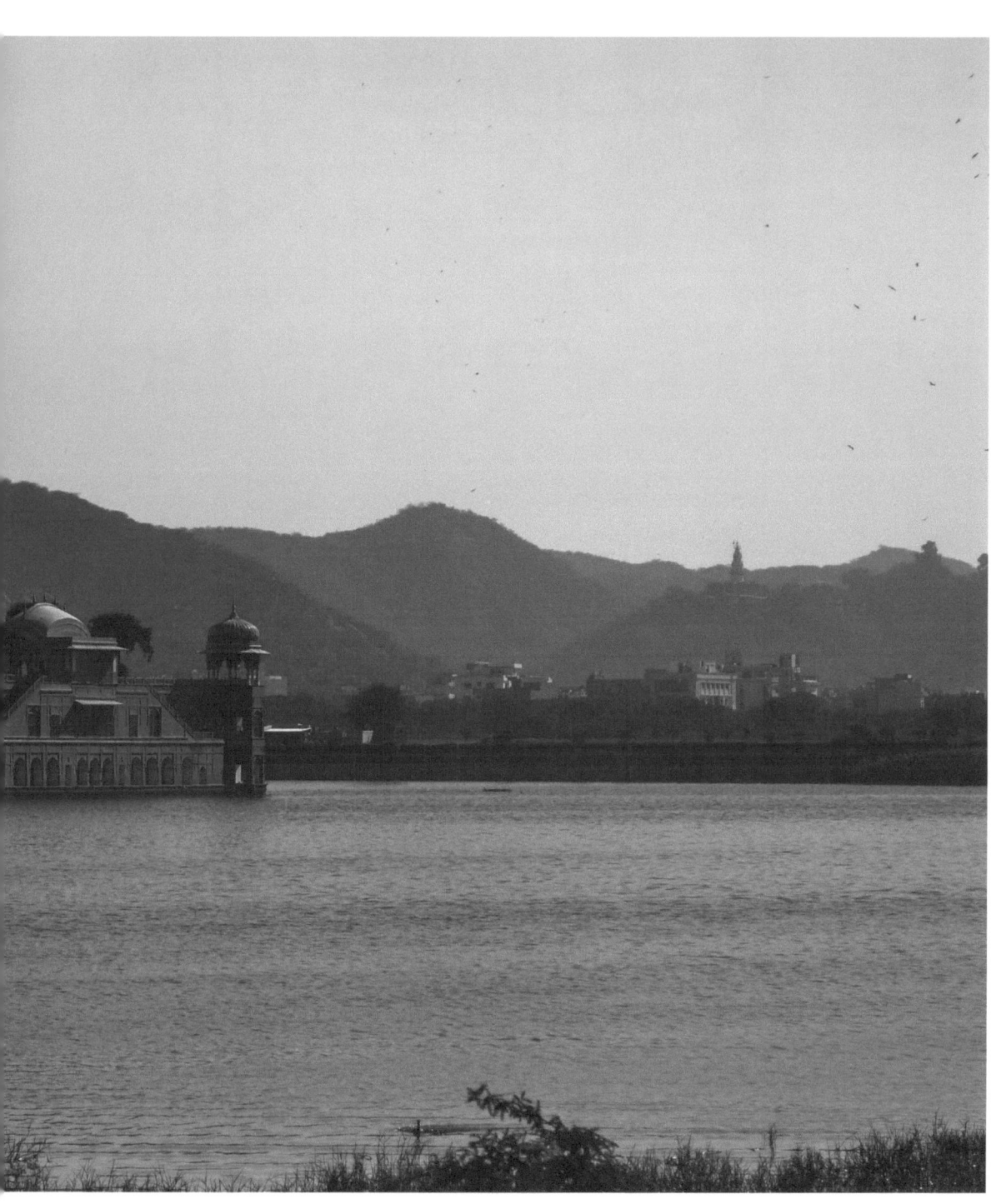

www.ingramcontent.com/pod-product-compliance
Lightning Source LLC
Chambersburg PA
CBHW040340250526
45473CB00046B/835